WITTGENSTEIN: A GUIDE FOR THE PERPLEXED

Also available from Continuum

WITTGENSTEIN: A GUIDE FOR THE PERPLEXED

MARK ADDIS

continuum

Continuum International Publishing Group
The Tower Building
11 York Road
London
SE1 7NX

80 Maiden Lane
Suite 704
New York, NY 10038

First published 2006
Reprinted 2007

British Library Cataloguing-in-Publication Data
A catalogue record for this book is available from the British Library.

ISBN-10: 0826484956 (hardback) 0826484964 (paperback)
ISBN-13: 9780826484956 (hardback) 9780826484963 (paperback)

Library of Congress Cataloging-in-Publication Data
Addis, Mark.
  Wittgenstein : a guide for the perplexed.
    p. cm.
  Includes bibliographical references (p.) and index.
  ISBN 0-8264-8495-6 (hardback) – ISBN 0-8264-8496-4 (pbk.)
  1. Wittgenstein, Ludwig, 1889–1951. I. Title.
  B3376.W564A644 2006
  192–dc22   2005024794

Typeset by Servis Filmsetting Limited, Manchester
Printed and bound in Great Britain by Biddles Ltd, King's Lynn, Norfolk

CONTENTS

PREFACE

Wittgenstein is one of the most important twentieth-century philosophers. The *Tractatus Logico-Philosophicus* and *Philosophical Investigations* have profoundly shaped the development of philosophy. Unlike some philosophers who are not well known outside the confines of the subject, Wittgenstein remains the focus of intense interest that extends far beyond philosophy. He occupies an influential place in contemporary thought but there is a lack of agreement about precisely what claims he made and the continuing weight which should be attributed to them. Any reasonably short introduction to Wittgenstein is inevitably selective. The objective of the guide is to equip readers with some of the requisite knowledge to better appreciate his approach and major ideas for themselves.

CHAPTER 1

INTRODUCTION

OVERVIEW

Wittgenstein is one of the most significant philosophers of the twentieth century. He radically challenged widely accepted views with powerful critiques that exposed the fundamental assumptions which underpinned them. Wittgenstein made notable original and controversial contributions to issues about the appropriate methodology for philosophy, and to the particular fields of language, logic, mathematics and mind, and epistemology. His writings[1] are divided into the phases of the early and later work. The later writings are usually classified further into the middle period, late period and (what is often termed) the Third Wittgenstein. Both his early and later work played a crucial role in the development of twentieth-century analytic philosophy.

Gottlob Frege (1848–1925) and Bertrand Russell (1872–1970) profoundly influenced Wittgenstein's early philosophy. The *Tractatus Logico-Philosophicus*[2] appeared in 1921 and was the only book that he published during his lifetime. It is presented in numbered sections which are hierarchically organized. The *Tractatus* emerged from Wittgenstein's *Notebooks 1914–1916* as a development of and reaction against the ideas about language and logic that Frege and Russell advocated. The work is founded upon the notion that problems in philosophy stem from a failure to understand language and it aimed to illuminate its essential character. Wittgenstein's employment of and philosophical attitudes to the newly invented logic of Frege and Russell was central to the *Tractatus*. The logical analysis presented in the book sought to resolve philosophical problems by reducing complex notions to their simple constituents. Wittgenstein provided a complex picture of the relations between language, logic and metaphysics. He claimed to have solved all the major problems of philosophy in the *Tractatus* and thereafter gave up philosophy until his return to the subject in 1929. Wittgenstein's renewal of interest in philosophy marks the start of the middle period which lasted until about 1935. He subjected the doctrines of the *Tractatus* to systematic criticism and began to develop many of the notions which are present in the *Philosophical Investigations*. Wittgenstein's concern with central themes of the *Tractatus* remained but he developed a radically new conception of language and rejected what he regarded as its dogmatic approach to philosophy. His conception of philosophy altered very significantly and he no longer thought that philosophical problems could be definitively and finally solved. Wittgenstein's approach to issues in philosophy eschewed logical analysis in favour of the description of linguistic usage. He claimed that philosophy should be viewed as a kind of therapy and that it should employ diverse methods which are akin to various therapies. The distinct stylistic changes between the *Tractatus* and middle period reflect these altered perspectives about language and the nature of philosophy. Between the start of the middle and the end of the late period around half of Wittgenstein's work dealt with the philosophy of mathematics. The first signs of what was to become a major interest in philosophy of mind clearly emerge towards the end of the middle period. Published works from this time include 'Some Remarks on Logical Form', *Ludwig Wittgenstein und der Wiener Kreis*, *Philosophical Remarks*, *Wittgenstein's Lectures: Cambridge 1930–2*, *Philosophical Grammar*, *Wittgenstein's Lectures: Cambridge 1932–5*, *Blue and Brown Books* and 'Wittgenstein's Notes for Lectures on "Private Experience" and "Sense Data"'.

The late period was from about 1936–45. Wittgenstein's most significant later work was the *Philosophical Investigations* and during the late period he devoted major attention to its preparation.[3] In 1945 part one of the *Investigations* was in its final manuscript form but Wittgenstein decided against publication. He only authorized its posthumous publication and the book appeared in 1953. In stylistic terms the *Investigations* resembles the middle period but the remarks in it are highly polished and condensed. The book moves from the discussion of one theme to another and lacks any easily identifiable structure. Such transition between topics is a consequence of Wittgenstein's view that an essential part of dissolving philosophical confusion is to approach errors from a variety of perspectives. Each time further sources of puzzlement are uncovered. Part one of the *Investigations* is concerned with a range of central philosophical problems, such as the nature of meaning and understanding, the character of propositions and of logic plus questions about states of consciousness and intentionality. Published works from this period include *Remarks on the Foundations of Mathematics, Lectures and Conversations on Aesthetics, Psychology and Religious Beliefs,* and *Wittgenstein's Lectures on the Foundations of Mathematics, Cambridge 1939.* There is a growing consensus that the period from 1946–51 comprised a distinct phase in Wittgenstein's thought (often termed the 'Third Wittgenstein'). Part two of the *Investigations* dates from this time and deals with issues in the philosophy of mind with a particular concentration upon aspect seeing. The best-known work of this period is *On Certainty* which contained Wittgenstein's most extensive and sustained discussions of epistemological questions. There is controversy over whether the writings in this period should be regarded as attempting to move in new directions from that of the *Investigations* or as a continuation of it. Published works from this period include *Zettel, Remarks on the Philosophy of Psychology, Last Writings on the Philosophy of Psychology, Culture and Value* and *Remarks on Colour.*

Sometimes introductions to Wittgenstein tend to present his ideas in a way which may encourage readers to think that he is much clearer and simpler than he actually is. An encounter with his writings soon dispels illusions of this kind and may leave readers wondering how to proceed when undertaking exegetical work of their own. It is useful to consider difficulties which typically arise when attempting to interpret Wittgenstein. The fact that interest in him extends beyond philosophy can promote the impression that no or very little prior background in the subject is required to understand him. Indeed the opposite is true and as with some other major figures, such as Kant, a sizeable amount of philosophical knowledge is demanded before he can be comprehended. In order to grasp the point of Wittgenstein's comments the targets of his criticism require identification. Since he did not specify them in a straightforward way, background knowledge is needed to ascertain what they actually are. A good grounding in the fields of the philosophies of language, logic, mathematics, mind and epistemology is valuable.

There is disagreement about the extent to which the details of Wittgenstein's life can be used to inform the comprehension of his philosophy. These divergences are especially evident when his philosophical influences are considered. One general position is that Wittgenstein was affected by another thinker if parallels between their ideas can be adduced. However, it might be objected that this standard for influence discards serious inquiry into the history of ideas by favouring the comparison of philosophical beliefs instead. What underlies this criticism is that if parallels are sufficiently broadly construed then it is difficult to conclude that the ascription of a particular thinker's influence is the most persuasive explanation of the origin of particular philosophical themes in Wittgenstein. It is important to exclude parallels which turn out to be simply coincidental when subjected to closer scrutiny. The position taken on the standard for philosophical influences upon him is likely to have a significant bearing on how exegesis is approached.

Serious exegesis requires appreciation of some issues raised by Wittgenstein's published works. He wrote copiously during his lifetime and since the 1960s his writings have steadily been published. Wittgenstein's manuscripts and typescripts, referred to as the *Nachlass*, have appeared as *Wittgenstein's Nachlass: The Bergen Electronic Edition* (2000). A complete edition of his correspondence, *Wittgenstein Gesamtbriefwechsel* (2004), came out recently. All his work is now in published form. Wittgenstein's texts with the exception of the *Tractatus* were compiled posthumously from *Nachlass* material. Arguably, some of the editing practices which were adopted have contributed to the difficulties of undertaking rigorous exegetical analysis. For example, Rhees compiled the *Philosophical Grammar* from sections of the original 'Big Typescript' and Wittgenstein's first two revisions of it.[4] Another instance is that Wittgenstein wrote the remarks which form part two of the *Investigations* between 1946–9 after he had completed the final manuscript form which he intended to submit for publication. He did not intend to include them in the book but the editors decided to. A general problem is that in many of Wittgenstein's published works passages from the part of the *Nachlass* from which the text has been drawn have been omitted. A difficulty these omissions create is that it is very hard to know whether the full context of a remark is being supplied without examining the *Nachlass*. For example, the 1968 version of 'Wittgenstein's Notes for Lectures on "Private

Experience" and "Sense Data"', edited by Rhees, omits passages[5] about mathematics which have been restored in the complete text of the 1993 edition. The omissions also have the consequence that it can be hard to make useful claims about the relationship between the texts from the middle period onwards, such as that between the *Philosophical Grammar* and *Investigations*. Improved editions of some of Wittgenstein's works have appeared and should be used whenever possible. The translations of Wittgenstein's writings have implications for exegesis. There are instances where the rendering of a passage is not entirely satisfactory and these tend to occur where a translator has imposed a particular interpretation on an especially difficult or obscure remark. In occasional cases, the same text may have more than one translation. The best-known case is that of the two translations of the *Tractatus*, firstly by C.K. Ogden (assisted by Frank Ramsey) and later by David Pears and Brian McGuinness.

Wittgenstein's writing has a literary quality rarely matched in German philosophical texts. He made use of metaphors, rhetorical questions, unexpected illustrations and other devices in order to make readers think. In his later work, Wittgenstein had a noticeable dislike of philosophical jargon because he thought that it obscured rather than clarified the nature of philosophical problems. However, he brought in his own terminology, such as 'language games' and 'family resemblance'. Wittgenstein was (almost) never satisfied with his own work and was constantly undertaking revisions which were quite often of a substantial kind. Part of his usual way of working was to reject some (or all) of his earlier thoughts upon a topic. Wittgenstein frequently rewrote remarks until they appeared in a form he was (more) satisfied with but what tended to happen in the process was that the context for understanding the remark (gradually) disappeared. The polished versions of the remarks are sometimes impenetrable and the arguments in favour of his insights fragmentary. Indeed, the styles of both the *Tractatus* and *Investigations* contribute to the major interpretative problems which they pose. Wittgenstein's inability or unwillingness to work his views into systematic and sustained lines of reasoning is a further source of difficulties. These problems about clarity and sustained argumentation coupled with the lack of straightforward identification of the targets of criticism quite frequently make it difficult to see the point of a remark or strategy. For example, consider the *Brown Book* where the purpose of imagining various linguistic situations is very infrequently elucidated and in its first 30 pages philosophy is mentioned just once. A related difficulty with the same causes is that of finding organizational and argumentative structure in his writings.

Having reflected on problems which typically arise when attempting to interpret Wittgenstein, it is now appropriate to see what the elements of a reliable exegetical methodology might well be. It is important when undertaking exegetical work to consider the relative authority of the texts. The *Tractatus* and *Investigations* have the highest standing (published and intended to be) followed by works which were compiled posthumously from *Nachlass* material. Those with the lowest authority are individuals' records of Wittgenstein's lectures and conversations. It is impossible to be sure that he said the precise words attributed to him. Knowledge of the circumstances of composition of Wittgenstein's work is valuable. Sometimes his letters provide useful information about this. An understanding of German is useful for reading any material which has not been translated and for checking published translations. Given Wittgenstein's style and the presentation of his ideas, it is perhaps not surprising that some of the (early) secondary literature has succumbed to the temptation to take individual remarks out of context to create a set of views which are attributed to him. This temptation must be resisted as experience shows that it leads to unsatisfactory readings of the texts. It is useful to check for variants of remarks through following references in published works to similar passages in other texts (and the *Nachlass* if being very thorough) as this helps to develop insight into the context of a remark. Examining the context of a remark can make producing an interpretation of it easier and if an interpretation fits the context this can be evidence in its favour. Compiling a list of occurrences of particular term(s) in Wittgenstein's writings is often useful when investigating a specific concept(s). Every mention of a term in the *Nachlass* can be found by using the electronic edition (2000). A key element of accurate exegesis is finding the structure and identifying the patterns which are present in Wittgenstein's work. Locating the order underlying particular arrangements of remarks helps to reveal argumentative contexts, strategies and moves. For example, although the *Investigations* seems to be haphazard and fragmentary in its composition, it is possible to divide it into distinct sections of text concerned with particular sets of issues. Recognizing patterns within Wittgenstein's writings could include those relating to the use of a specific term or notion, such as regularly being found in conjunction with another concept, and to his use of particular typographical devices. For instance, Baker's articles 'Italics in Wittgenstein' (1999) and 'Quotation-marks in the *Philosophical Investigations* Part I' (2002) provide guidance about how to approach typographical pattern identification. In the former he was concerned to investigate the standard view that italics are always used for emphasis. Patterns which were identified include italics to indicate purpose specific explanations or back references or to register a particular sense of a concept. Baker suggested that in many cases italics are equivalent to the use of single quotation marks.

There is a huge and steadily growing secondary literature about Wittgenstein. An efficient way to search this is to use the database *Philosopher's Index*. The interpretative difficulties about Wittgenstein's writings already discussed manifest themselves in the controversy over and the wide variations in the understanding of his work. Claims by scholars that other commentators have misrepresented what a particular philosopher thought may indeed arise from identifications of exegetical errors but they may also be expressions of an alternative perspective. Distinguishing between these reasons for alleged misinterpretation is a particularly significant task when appraising the literature on Wittgenstein. Commentaries on the *Tractatus* and *Investigations* are particularly useful for facilitating deeper study. They provide systematic analysis of the texts including discussion of the development of his ideas and the original context of compressed remarks.

BIOGRAPHY

Ludwig Josef Johann Wittgenstein was born in Vienna on 26 April 1889.[6] For several generations both sides of his family had been wealthy and cultured. Wittgenstein's paternal grandfather was a successful wool merchant. He was Jewish but converted to Protestantism and married the daughter of a banker. They became established supporters of the arts and provided their son Karl with a classical education. However, this kind of education did not suit him and aged 17 he went to America where he supported himself for two years. Upon his return to Vienna he was granted his wish to study engineering which was where his real interests and talent lay. In less than 30 years he had become the leading figure in the iron and steel industry of the Austro-Hungarian Empire and one of its wealthiest citizens. Wittgenstein's maternal grandfather was descended from a prominent Jewish family but had been raised as a Catholic, and had married one. In 1873, Karl married their daughter, Leopoldine Kalmus, and they had eight children with Wittgenstein being the youngest. All were baptized as Catholics. Leopoldine strongly encouraged cultural and especially musical activities and the family was important in Viennese cultural circles. Wittgenstein's brother Paul was a concert pianist. Wittgenstein himself had fine musical sensitivity but did not appreciate pieces later than Brahms. By the standards of his gifted family, Wittgenstein displayed no particular aptitudes as a boy. However, he did show considerable manual dexterity when he created a working model of a sewing machine.

Karl had somewhat eccentric ideas about education which may have been shaped by his experiences. He was determined that his elder sons should contribute to the running of his business empire and they were given a private education designed to enable them to cope with the demands of commerce. From 1903–6 Wittgenstein went to the *Realschule* in Linz. The school was more technical and less academic than a grammar school. Part of the motivation for the choice was the concern that he would fail a demanding entrance examination for a grammar school. However, the main consideration was that his interests would be better served by a technically orientated education but he was not happy there. Wittgenstein had been interested in studying with Boltzmann who was Professor of Physics at the University of Vienna but he committed suicide in 1906. Instead Wittgenstein studied mechanical engineering at the Technische Hochschule at Charlottenburg in Berlin as it had been decided that his technical knowledge should be improved. Wittgenstein attended for three terms and was awarded his diploma in 1908. Photographs of the time indicate that he was impeccably dressed and much concerned about his appearance.

Although Wittgenstein had developed an interest in aeronautical engineering he was increasingly fascinated by philosophical problems. In 1908 he left for England and during the summer of that year he flew experimental kites at the Kite Flying Upper Atmosphere Station near Glossop in Derbyshire. From that autumn until 1911 he was registered as research student in aeronautical engineering at Manchester University. Wittgenstein was working on the design and construction of an aircraft engine. The concept was to rotate the propeller of the engine using high-speed gases from a combustion chamber. Wittgenstein became interested in the mathematical features of the design, then by mathematics itself and ultimately by philosophical problems concerning the foundations of mathematics. He was introduced to Russell's *The Principles of Mathematics*. This work covered recent advances in logic and the foundations of mathematics made by Russell himself and Frege. It had a significant impact upon him. Wittgenstein had found a field which absorbed him and to which he sought to make a major contribution.

Wittgenstein met Frege at Jena in 1911 for advice about pursuing his interests. Frege recommended that he should study with Russell at Cambridge University. From 1912–13 he registered as a student. Russell was his supervisor and they discussed logic and philosophy with Wittgenstein's ability soon becoming apparent. By this time the preoccupations with the pursuit of perfection in philosophy and personal morality which fundamentally shaped his life had begun to manifest themselves. For example, in 1912 Wittgenstein's conversations with Russell featured his doubts about his personal moral worth and the need for change as much as logical and philosophical issues. The relationship between Wittgenstein and Russell rapidly transformed into one between colleagues. The latter remarked '. . . he will solve the problems I am too old to solve – all kinds of problems that are raised by my work, but want a fresh mind and the vigour of youth. He is *the* young man one hopes for' (letter to Ottoline Morrell 22.03.1912). In 1912 Wittgenstein went to Iceland with David Pinsent and the following year they visited Norway. He received a substantial inheritance when his father died in January 1913. Wittgenstein felt that his philosophical work required solitude and later in 1913 he returned to Norway where he lodged in the village of Skjolden where he undertook research in logic. Wittgenstein briefly visited Vienna at Christmas 1913. In April 1914 Moore (1873–1958) came to see him and took a series of dictations about logic.

Wittgenstein returned to Austria around the end of June 1914 and once war was declared he volunteered for the Austro-Hungarian army straightaway. During the war his efforts were directed towards the problems in the *Tractatus*. Religion was an important concern for Wittgenstein although he was not religious in a conventional kind of way. In September 1914 Wittgenstein encountered Tolstoy's *Gospel in Brief* and was profoundly affected by it. From 1914–16 he was a technician in an artillery workshop stationed firstly in Krakow and then

Sokal. In 1916 Wittgenstein was sent to Olmütz for officer training. He met Paul Engelmann and they talked about religious matters.[7] In January 1917 Wittgenstein was posted back to the Eastern front as an artillery officer and in February 1918 he joined a mountain artillery regiment on the Italian front. During these two years he was awarded two medals for valour. In August 1918 the *Tractatus* manuscript was completed. In November the Austro-Hungarian war effort fell apart and the Italians took about half a million prisoners of war – including Wittgenstein. During his imprisonment in a camp in Cassino he decided to train as an elementary school teacher. In a letter of March 1919 Wittgenstein informed Russell that he had a finished *Tractatus* manuscript. John Maynard Keynes used his political influence to allow Wittgenstein to send a copy of it to Russell. Wittgenstein claimed to have solved all the major problems of philosophy in the *Tractatus* and thereafter gave up philosophy until his return to the subject in 1929. In August 1919 he was released from the camp.

Wittgenstein's war service had a significant effect on his attitudes to life, especially with regard to wealth and lifestyle. He decided to make a radical break with his past and live in a fundamentally different way. Wittgenstein insisted upon donating his entire inheritance to his siblings in September 1919. From then onwards he lived completely simply and without ornament. In the same month he enrolled on a one-year course in primary school teaching. He and Russell discussed the *Tractatus* line by line at a meeting in Holland in December 1919. Russell agreed to contribute an introduction to it. He claimed that it 'certainly deserves, by its breadth and scope and profundity, to be considered an important event in the philosophical world' (*TLP*, p. 7). When Wittgenstein saw Russell's introduction he complained that Russell had misunderstood his views and misrepresented them (*LWCL*, p. 152). Wittgenstein made several attempts to publish the book but none of them succeeded. He graduated from the teaching course in July 1920 and in despair left the matter of publication to Russell. The *Tractatus* was first published in German in 1921 and in English in 1922.

In autumn 1920 Wittgenstein began as schoolmaster in the village of Trattenbach which lay in the hills south of Vienna but became increasingly unhappy there. In November 1922 he transferred to Puchberg in the Schneeberg mountains. Ramsey was a young mathematician of outstanding promise who had assisted with the

English translation of the *Tractatus* and reviewed it for the journal *Mind*. He took up Wittgenstein's invitation to visit in September 1923, when the *Tractatus* was discussed in detail, and in May 1924. However, Ramsey could not persuade Wittgenstein to resume his philosophical work. Difficulties arose at Puchberg and he transferred again to the village of Otterthal in September 1924. Whilst there he wrote and published a spelling dictionary for use in elementary schools. In all his teaching positions, Wittgenstein's high expectations and stern measures for enforcing them had upset the majority of his pupils and invoked the hostility of their parents. After a complaint about his treatment of a pupil Wittgenstein decided to resign his post in April 1926. (At the subsequent hearing about the incident he was cleared of misconduct.) He was deeply dejected at the failure of his teaching venture.

Wittgenstein worked as a gardener at a monastery in Hütteldorf outside Vienna and at the end of the summer in 1926 he returned to the city. His sister Gretl and her architect Engelmann asked him to become a partner in the design and construction of her new house. Although the early plans were drawn up collaboratively, once Wittgenstein was a partner he assumed control of the interior design. He admired the work of Adolf Loos and that influence is evident in the stark modern style of the house. Wittgenstein paid tremendous attention to every detail of the building. For example, the seemingly simple radiators took a year to deliver because the sort of thing Wittgenstein envisaged could not be constructed in Austria. Gretl moved into the house at the end of 1928. Through work on the building Wittgenstein returned to Viennese social life and thereby eventually philosophy. Moritz Schlick was Professor of the History and Philosophy of the Inductive Sciences at Vienna University. He was the founder of a circle (which evolved into the Vienna Circle) of philosophers and mathematicians who were united in their positivist approach to philosophical problems and scientific world view. Schlick sought out Wittgenstein because he admired him and they first met early in 1927. Schlick did not succeed in drawing Wittgenstein into the circle itself. However, by summer 1927 he was meeting regularly with a group which included Schlick and carefully selected members of his circle including Friedrich Waismann, Rudolf Carnap and Herbert Feigl. As Wittgenstein regained interest in philosophy he realized that the *Tractatus* had not solved all its major problems. The recognition of this was the stimulus for his later philosophy.

The revival of Wittgenstein's philosophical concerns led to a return to Cambridge University in January 1929. By now the *Tractatus* was internationally regarded as a philosophical classic and he found out that it could be submitted for a doctoral degree. Wittgenstein registered with Ramsey as a supervisor. Russell and Moore were the examiners and he received the degree in June of that year. He required funding to be able to carry on with his philosophical work and set about securing a position at Cambridge. At the end of Michaelmas term 1930 he was awarded a five-year Fellowship at Trinity College with the typescript which was posthumously published as the *Philosophical Remarks* being accepted as a fellowship dissertation. Wittgenstein began delivering lectures which were not all academic in style. He usually held them in his rooms. Wittgenstein did not use notes but instead thought before the class and gave an impression of tremendous concentration. Whether the discussion became productive greatly depended upon the audience. Wittgenstein considered rejecting academic life entirely and going, with Francis Skinner, to reside in the Soviet Union where they would seek manual labouring work. His motives for wishing to go there primarily stemmed from his belief about the simple ascetic kind of life being led there and to a lesser extent from his passionate admiration of Tolstoy's moral teachings and Dostoevsky's spiritual insights. He and Skinner had been taking Russian lessons since the start of 1934 in preparation for their visit to the Soviet Union.[8] Wittgenstein travelled there in September 1935 but eventually decided against emigration because it became clear to him that he would not be permitted to settle there as a manual worker.

Wittgenstein went to Skjolden in Norway in August 1936. He aimed to use the *Brown Book* as the basis for the preparation of a final formulation of his intended book. This was part of one of his attempts to mould his work into a suitable shape but by November he had abandoned this attempt at revision. Immediately afterwards Wittgenstein started those manuscripts which eventually led to the *Investigations*. His concern with perfection in personal morality was particularly strong at this time. When Wittgenstein visited Vienna and England around New Year in 1937 he confessed to several of his friends about times in his life when he had been weak and dishonest in order to dismantle the pride which had produced his weakness. He was in Norway between August and December 1937. Through correspondence with Sraffa, Wittgenstein became aware of his position following the *Anschluss* between Germany and Austria in March 1938. He travelled to Cambridge in that month with the intention of seeking a post at the university. Wittgenstein resumed teaching activities more regularly and received some payment for the academic year 1938–9. In February 1939 he succeeded Moore as Professor of Philosophy and in June became a British citizen. Wittgenstein's lectures on the foundations of mathematics in 1939 were partly notable for having Alan Turing, a distinguished twentieth-century mathematician, in the audience. In 1941 he volunteered to work as a porter and laboratory technician in Guy's Hospital in London and in 1943 he joined a team working on the physiology of shock at the Royal Victoria Infirmary in Newcastle as a research technician.

In February 1944 Wittgenstein left for an extended stay in Swansea and in the October he returned to Cambridge. His hostility towards professional philosophy and his dislike of Cambridge remained constant throughout his academic career. Wittgenstein continued his duties until August 1947 when he resigned his Chair to concentrate on his writing. The university awarded him Michealmas term as a period of sabbatical leave so he formally ceased to be a professor at the end of the year. In 1948 Wittgenstein went to Ireland, living for part of the time in a cottage in Connemara and spent the winter of that year in Ross's Hotel in Dublin. He suffered from ill health and after returning from a visit to the United States in October 1949 he was diagnosed with prostate cancer. From then onwards Wittgenstein lived with various friends in Oxford and Cambridge. Health permitting he continued work actively at philosophy until virtually the end of his life. He died in Cambridge on 29 April 1951. His last words were 'tell them I've had a wonderful life'.

WITTGENSTEIN'S PHILOSOPHICAL INFLUENCE

Questions about Wittgenstein's place in twentieth-century analytic and continental philosophy and selected aspects of the significance of his writings for some other disciplines are very briefly considered. The aim is to draw some of the broad contours of his influence so that the reader can profitably approach specialist works about this, such as Hacker's *Wittgenstein's Place in Twentieth Century Analytical Philosophy* (1996b). The fields to which his work has been applied include the philosophies of language, logic, mind, cognitive science, mathematics, religion, aesthetics, ethics, political and social philosophy, and jurisprudence. The precise nature and scope of Wittgenstein's importance remains a subject of controversy. Disagreements over this continue to have an impact on contemporary philosophical practice. Wittgenstein's work is an integral part of mainstream twentieth-century analytic philosophy and he was central to its development between the 1930s and 1970s. Russell expressed Wittgenstein's significance when he remarked (1959, p. 216) that 'during the period since 1914 three philosophies have successively dominated the British philosophical world, first that of Wittgenstein's *Tractatus*, second that of the Logical Positivists, and third that of Wittgenstein's *Philosophical Investigations*'. This appraisal is largely accurate but its scope is rather too narrow as Wittgenstein shaped analytic philosophy internationally.

The Vienna Circle was greatly influenced by the *Tractatus* but their adoption of its major concepts was selective. The Circle rejected the picture theory of meaning, the distinction between saying and showing, plus most of the metaphysics of logical atomism. However, they accepted the ideas of the *Tractatus* about the character and limits of philosophy (as an activity of clarification), the conception of logic (as analytic) and logical necessity as well as the notion of the logical analysis of language. The subsequent use and indeed misuse of these ideas had a profound effect upon the views of the Circle. The *Tractatus* significantly shaped the direction of the philosophy of language, especially with regard to the objective of creating a theory of meaning for natural language. The goal of producing such a theory shares a number of fundamental presuppositions with that work. One of these is that in all natural languages the conjunction of a system of rules with assignments of meaning together fix the meaning of every grammatical (that is, well-formed) sentence in the language. Taken together with appropriate facts, this calculus of meaning unequivocally determines the truth value of each sentence. Another is that the grammar of natural language hides the complex system of rules which underpins it and that these rules can be exposed by analysis.

From the 1930s onwards Wittgenstein's middle period and later work were of pivotal importance to the course of analytic philosophy. He initially affected its development through his series of lectures. Members of the audience included philosophers, such as Malcolm, who would later elucidate and apply Wittgenstein's views to a substantial range of issues. The posthumous publication of the *Investigations* and a steady stream of other writings augmented his influence. Prior to this Wittgenstein's major works of the later period had not been directly available to philosophers and they had relied upon, for example, lecture notes from his students. He systematically criticized the presuppositions about language and logic which underpinned the *Tractatus* and in doing so also repudiated basic suppositions of the project of creating a theory of meaning for natural language. A prominent criticism was that of the idea that words are the names of objects and the meaning of each one is the object which it stands for. Wittgenstein's criticism was coupled with the introduction of new conceptions of language, many of which gained widespread currency. One of these is the idea that the use of language is an important part of meaning. His thinking about language particularly influenced what is termed ordinary language philosophy (of which Ryle was an exemplary representative). Ordinary language philosophy directed its attention towards the ordinary use of linguistic expressions and the discovery of the informal logic which governed the rules for their employment. This approach to philosophy gradually declined in influence. Another aspect of Wittgenstein's work which had an extremely significant impact was that in the philosophy of mind. He developed a deep and comprehensive criticism of the picture of the relationship between the physical and the mental which has been dominant since Descartes. Essentially the picture is that an individual has privileged access to the contents of his mind whilst others can only ever indirectly access his mental phenomena through bodily and behavioural manifestations. The most significant critique of this conception was the private language argument which aimed to demonstrate that a language of this kind is not possible.

Interest in Wittgenstein and scholarship about his writings has flourished since the 1960s. However, from then onwards he became less influential in analytic philosophy generally as his critical stance towards the use of theory and science in philosophy gradually fell out of favour. A major reason for this was the dominance of a scientific conception of philosophy in the United States (which had emerged as the centre of Anglophone analytic philosophy by the mid-1970s). Another significant factor was that the perspective on language espoused by the *Investigations* was supplanted by theories of meaning which had affinities with the *Tractatus*, and that were complemented by developments in (Chomskian) theoretical linguistics. Wittgenstein's philosophy of mind lost ground to materialist conceptions which drew strength from work in neuroscience and to the construal of the operations of the mind and brain on a functionalist model that were promoted by the rise of the computer. At present Wittgenstein is somewhat unfashionable. These historical developments raise the question of whether Wittgenstein should justifiably be regarded as the single most influential twentieth-century analytic philosopher. This issue is contentious as it is hard to judge the importance of recent philosophers and no substantial consensus about it has emerged so far.

The recent decline in Wittgenstein's influence brings up the matter of whether this reflects an appropriate assessment of the value of his philosophical methodology or rather a failure to understand the full significance of his approach. His view was that philosophical problems are dissolved by showing how they are created by linguistic abuses and that what is required is a description of the grammar of language. The majority of twentieth-century analytic philosophy has not accepted Wittgenstein's position that the source of philosophical problems is linguistic confusion. Rather, it has indicated a greater adherence to the philosophical legacy of Frege and Russell than Wittgenstein, and has devoted systematic attention to what accepted tradition characterizes as the problems of philosophy. Wittgenstein differed radically from this tradition because of his conception of philosophical methodology. For example, he went against this tradition in not sharply distinguishing between epistemology and metaphysics since given his conception of philosophy there would be little to be gained by a precise differentiation between the two. The prevalent response to criticisms of Wittgenstein's philosophical methodology is to claim that many analytic philosophers systematically misinterpret him and that a proper understanding of him would change their perspective. Similarly, it is maintained that a large proportion of the arguments which are widely held to have refuted Wittgenstein's approach in certain areas, such as in the philosophy of mind, are either founded on misunderstanding or are inconclusive. It remains to be seen whether he will once again dominate the practice of analytical philosophy.

Wittgenstein had a far less significant place in the twentieth-century continental philosophical tradition than in the analytic one. However, a recent trend has been a lessening of the divide between analytical and continental philosophy, and their growing convergence has promoted interest in Wittgenstein's work. His work has been incorporated into continental philosophy with a prominent example of this being the misuse[9] of his ideas by Jean-François Lyotard (1924–88) in his highly influential formulation of postmodernism in *The Postmodern Condition*. In his investigation of the problem of the legitimization of knowledge Lyotard employed his version of Wittgenstein's notion of language games. According to Lyotard the theory of these games enabled the definition of various types of utterance in terms of rules specifying their properties and the uses to which they can be put. He claimed that the rules of language games do not legitimate themselves but are subject to agreement between their players and that without rules there is no game (with every change in them altering the game). Every utterance is a move in a language game and each different type pertains to a distinct kind of language game. Lyotard drew the conclusion that these games are incommensurable and presented a postmodern methodological representation of society as composed of multifarious and fragmented language games in which each one strictly controls the moves which can be made within it. Another increasing area of interest is that of the relationship between Wittgenstein's work and that of continental philosophers. For instance, a growing number of commentators have suggested that his treatment of meaning and understanding could be viewed in terms drawn from Derrida.[10] It is argued that both took metaphysics as a primary target and focused upon what they regarded as a dubious concept of the mental self presence of meanings. The origin of this questionable concept is the attempt to explain how it is possible to represent meaning in the signs of language if it is assumed that what could account for this has to be located in the mind. Wittgenstein is interpreted as adopting a consistently deconstructive perspective. The writing in the *Investigations* is a kind of deconstructive syntax which is aimed like Derrida's against a predominant philosophical concern with the nature of things.

Wittgenstein's philosophy has influenced other fields including linguistics, literary studies, sociology, religion, psychology and cognitive science. Linguistic critiques inspired by his work have sought to expose the spurious nature of the central question of linguistic theory which is that of how it is possible to understand sentences which have not been heard previously. The theories which are challenged emanate both from theoretical linguistics and the philosophy of language in the Frege and Russell tradition (such as that propounded by

Davidson). For example, there are analogies between the *Tractatus* idea of the forms of logical syntax which govern all possible languages being disguised by natural language and Chomsky's conception of the deep structure of language in which hidden grammatical rules and patterns of grammatical transformation were uncovered. The perspectives offered by these linguistic theories is that problems of how linguistic creativity is possible are tackled by the creation of a theory of meaning for language. Scientific investigations aided by philosophical analysis will demonstrate that language is a complex system of rules that are tacitly known to speakers. Some of the major assumptions employed include the distinction between sense and force and the characterization of meaning in terms of truth or assertion conditions. Wittgensteinian criticisms argue that these presuppositions are incoherent and thus any theory which utilizes them is unsatisfactory. Philosophical problems will not be solved by new insights into language and its associated mental phenomena but by clearly describing its use.

At present Wittgenstein's writings have had a limited impact upon disciplines which are concerned with the theory and practice of criticism of the arts but this is beginning to change. A number of scholars have suggested that the implications of his later work for such criticism should be explored, particularly with regard to the explanatory role of theory. Wittgensteinian critiques of the theory and practice of criticism of the arts focus upon the clarification of appropriate kinds of explanation and argue that theory should not be one of these. For example, his philosophical methodology has been applied to expose conceptual confusion in prominent theories such as psychoanalysis, cognitive psychology and structuralism. In the field of literary studies Wittgenstein's work has been related to the theory and philosophy of literature. Attention has been devoted to topics such as the links between ethics and literature, the character of poetic language, and the semantic analysis of fictional discourse.

The social sciences (considered as a single group) have been influenced by Wittgenstein's writings. A seminal early work which explored the connections between them was Peter Winch's *The Idea of a Social Science* and much later work in this area has continued to investigate the same kinds of questions. Wittgensteinian critiques of the methodologies for social science centre around issues about what kind of understanding is possible and which forms of explanation are legitimate. They argue that the relationship between the social sciences and philosophy is misunderstood because the nature of philosophy itself is misconceived. A major target of criticism is the advocacy of a positivist approach to social science which claims that these disciplines could be truly scientific if it was possible to incorporate the causal explanatory methods of natural science. Wittgenstein-inspired criticisms maintain that these methods of causal explanation are wholly inappropriate in social science. The concept of forms of life which is found in Wittgenstein is employed to develop the idea that notions which are used by a society may only be interpreted in the context of the particular form of life of that society. What is required is a description of these notions.

The contribution which Wittgenstein's work has made to religious studies and theology is highly controversial. It is argued that he developed a distinctive way of understanding religious belief which is consonant with not regarding religion as just a kind of superstition or irrationality. As such Wittgenstein's perspective is opposed to the idea that philosophical investigation can undermine various traditional claims which religion makes about the nature of reality. Wittgenstein's remarks about religion and magic emphasized the distinctive character of religious language and how it can be misunderstood if its presuppositions are regarded as alternatives to scientific ones. Some scholars claim that his work has important implications for theological issues about how the self is conceived. This is because modern theology often employs a Cartesian view of the self which functions as an autonomous and rational consciousness, and this picture of the self is one of the targets of criticism in Wittgenstein's private language argument. In the case of theological debates about the immortality of the soul, it has been claimed that he thought the attempt to prove this was nonsensical and involved a deep misunderstanding of both religious belief and the role of assertions about the soul. It has been suggested that Wittgenstein's discussion of forms of life and of the place of ritual may be useful in elucidating how a believer relates to religious institutions and established practices.

In psychology and cognitive science Wittgenstein's work has been used to develop critiques of existing theories and practices. Such criticisms argue that the investigation of topics in these disciplines raises many misleading pictures and potential sources of confusion. It is claimed that a significant number of psychological and cognitive science theories have conceptual problems. (These possible confusions also apply to accounts in philosophy of language and theoretical linguistics if they incorporate positions about psychological notions.) For example, many contemporary theories of perception, memory, imagination, emotion and volition are alleged to have embedded conceptual confusions. Wittgensteinian critiques maintain that his philosophy of mind is relevant to both the development and practice of psychology and cognitive science as sciences. This is because empirical theories in these fields take the ordinary use of psychological concepts for granted. For example, theories of perception presume the ordinary concept of perception which is characterized by the grammatical features of words like 'seeing'. Descriptions of the relationships between concepts, such as that between perception and sensation, should be clarified and the structure of connections between distinct conceptual domains, like the mental and behavioural, should be articulated. Such critiques argue that conceptual muddles about how the brain is related to the mind have an effect upon what form legitimate investigation in psychology and cognitive science should take in terms of how the issues are framed, results are interpreted, and conclusions drawn.

CHAPTER 2

CHARTING THE BOUNDS OF SENSE

GENESIS OF THE *TRACTATUS*

The *Tractatus* raises significant problems about how individual remarks and the book as a whole should be interpreted. General difficulties with Wittgenstein's writings arising from his literary style, the gradual loss of context surrounding comments, and the lack of systematic and sustained argumentation are major contributory factors. A number of technical terms, such as elementary proposition, and their interconnections need to be grasped. Virtually every remark in the work requires additional elucidation before it can be properly understood. Wittgenstein's *Notebooks 1914–1916* are valuable for resolving exegetical questions since the book emerged from them. A problem particular to the *Tractatus* stems from its division into a series of numbered paragraphs. The avowed purpose of this is to indicate the importance of a proposition through the decimal number that is assigned to it. Paragraph n.1 (and so on) is a further elucidation of proposition number n and propositions n.m1, n.m2 (and so on) are further elucidations of proposition number n.m, and so on. For instance, 1.11 is a comment upon 1.1. The seven fundamental propositions which the work is constructed from are ascribed whole numbers starting with 'The world is everything that is the case' (1) and ending on 'Whereof one cannot speak, thereof one must be silent' (7). These propositions are best regarded as indicative content headings. Difficulties are created by the fact that Wittgenstein did not employ this numbering system in a consistent fashion.

Wittgenstein was fundamentally influenced by Frege and Russell. Evidence of this is manifested throughout the *Tractatus* beginning with the preface (p. 29): 'I will only mention that to the great works of Frege and the writings of my friend Bertrand Russell I owe in large measure the stimulation of my thoughts'. Their work essentially defines the philosophical problems which are addressed in the book. The *Tractatus* is simultaneously a development of and reaction against the conceptions of language and logic which Frege and Russell propounded. They were convinced that philosophical progress could be achieved via the employment of logical analysis which aimed to reduce complex concepts to their elements. The commitment to and use of this kind of analysis is central to the *Tractatus*. Frege and Russell had recently invented modern formal (or mathematical) logic and this logic played a crucial role in the detailed construction of the doctrines in the book. Their importance for the *Tractatus* is unquestioned but it remains a matter of controversy how its claims relate to theirs.

It is appropriate to briefly consider certain basic aspects of Frege's and Russell's contributions to the development of logic and analytic philosophy which are germane to the *Tractatus*. The notion of a foundation for mathematics is essentially the idea that all acceptable mathematics ought to have certain specified properties (where this includes practices, methods, and so on). Frege and Russell were concerned that the mathematics of their time rested on inadequate foundations and they sought to place mathematics on a sound logical basis. The objective of their work was to prove the correctness of logicism which roughly speaking is the idea that mathematics is in some important sense reducible to logic. This involved demonstrating that all mathematical truths can be translated into logical truths and that the theorems of mathematics belong to those of logic. Frege was extremely careful about the proper description and definition of logical and mathematical concepts. He sought a logical system which could be used to resolve mathematical statements in terms of simpler logical notions. Frege essentially reconceived the discipline of logic by constructing a formal system which effectively constituted the first predicate calculus. This enabled the representation of valid inferences between propositions in which properties are predicated of objects. The system is the foundation of the modern predicate calculus. Frege formalized the notion of proof. His method consisted of a set of logical axioms and a set of rules of inference that laid out the conditions under which certain propositions may be correctly inferred from others. Frege showed how every step in the proof of a proposition was justified either in terms of one of the axioms or one of the rules of inference or by a theorem or derived rule that had already been proved.

Frege's great contribution to logic was to introduce various mathematical elements into logic. He formalized the theory of inference in a way which was at once more rigorous and more general in its application than traditional Aristotelian logic. He freed himself from the limitations of the subject and predicate analysis of natural language sentences that formed its basis. In this logic the subject and direct object of a sentence are not on a logical par. The rules governing the inferences between statements with different but related subject terms are different from the rules governing the inferences between statements with different but related verb complements. For example, the rule which permits the valid inference from 'Caesar conquered Gaul' to 'Something conquered Gaul' is different from the rule which permits the valid inference from 'Caesar conquered Gaul' to 'Caesar conquered something'. In Aristotelian logic, these inferences have nothing in common. Frege replaced the grammatical distinction between subject and predicate by one between function and argument. An argument is a variable substitution in a function. If a function only takes one argument this will be indicated by a single variable, two arguments are indicated by two variables and so on. Functions take arguments and map those arguments to a value. For instance, the value of the function $x + 1$ for the argument 2 is 3. Frege extended the applicability of his logic to the representation of non-mathematical predicates. There is no logical difference between the subject and direct object of a sentence. Incomplete expressions signifying functions are called predicates in a logical rather than a grammatical sense. For instance, the predicate 'conquered' denotes a function of two variables taking the arguments 'Caesar' and 'Gaul'. The truth value is the value of the function for different arguments and it is always either the True or the False. For example, the sentence 'Caesar conquered Gaul' denotes the True. Concepts are treated as functions which map arguments to one of the truth values. Frege produced a more general treatment of inferences involving 'all' and 'some' by treating these quantifiers as variable binding operators. Regardless of where the quantified expression appeared it was to be handled in the same way.

Demonstrating the correctness of logicism was the objective of Frege's *Grundgesetze der Arithmetic* and of Russell and Whitehead's three-volume *Principia Mathematica* (1910–13). Their basic idea for defending logicism was that numbers may be identified with classes of classes and that statements about numbers may be explained in terms of quantifiers and identity. Thus the number 1 would be identified with the class of all one-membered classes, the number 2 with the class of all two-membered classes, and so on. Propositions such as 'there are two books' would be recast as statements such as 'there is a book, x, and there is a book, y, and x is not identical to y'. In the *Grundgesetze*, Frege thought that he had shown that mathematics is in some important sense reducible to logic but the logical system he employed contained a disastrous defect. Russell discovered this flaw when he formulated the paradox that bears his name in 1901. He notified Frege in 1902 just as the second volume of the *Grundgesetze* was going to press. The paradox arises in connection with the set of all sets that are not members of themselves. Such a set, if it exists, will be a member of itself if and only if it is not a member of itself. The paradox is significant since, using classical logic, all sentences are entailed by a contradiction. Russell's response to this paradox came with the development of his 'simple' theory of types in his *Principles of Mathematics* (1903). It was clear to Russell that some restrictions should be placed upon the original axiom of naive set theory that formalizes the intuition that any coherent condition may be employed to determine a set. Russell's fundamental idea was that his paradox could be avoided by arranging all propositions into a hierarchy. He began with propositions about individuals at the lowest level followed by those about sets of individuals at the next and propositions about sets of sets of individuals at the next, and so on. All objects for which a given condition holds must be at the same level or of the same 'type'. The simple theory of types was further developed by Russell to become the 'ramified' theory in his 1908 article 'Mathematical logic as based on the theory of types' (Russell, 1956a) and in *Principia Mathematica*. Both the simple and ramified versions were criticized for being too weak since they failed to resolve all known paradoxes and for being too strong since they disallowed many mathematical definitions which were actually consistent. Wittgenstein was deeply dissatisfied by the theory of types and much of his work in logic was motivated by a wish to find a good alternative to it.

Wittgenstein accepted Frege's commitment to the determinacy of sense in the *Tractatus*. The requirement that sense must be determinate featured prominently in Frege's logic as an ideal which a logically perfect language must attain but natural languages do not satisfy. His principle of completeness of definition required of the explanation of a concept word that it solely fixes for every object whether or not each object comes under the concept. One formulation of this principle was as a metaphorical characterization of a concept as a sharp boundary drawn on an infinite plane which was compared to an area (1962, §56). Frege introduced the equality sign '=' into logic from mathematics and employed it with the meaning of identical with. This introduction in conjunction with his view that sense is determinate prompted his interest in philosophical problems concerned with sense and reference. In 'On sense and reference' Frege (1980) considered a puzzle about how to account for the difference in cognitive significance between identity statements when they are true. For example, 'the morning star is identical to the morning star' is true simply by inspection but 'the morning star is identical to the evening star' is not. Frege claimed that the words of a language have both a sense and a reference. The sense of an expression accounts for its cognitive significance. For instance, the descriptions 'the morning star' and 'the evening star' refer to the planet Venus but have different senses which express different ways of conceiving of Venus. Wittgenstein employed the terms 'sense' and 'reference' in a technical way although he disagreed with several aspects of Frege's theory of meaning.

Wittgenstein shared Frege and Russell's commitment to anti-psychologism and accepted its main tenets. He remarked that 'psychology is no more closely related to philosophy than to any other natural science' (*TLP*, 4.1121). The main goal of anti-psychologism was to ensure that logic, mathematics, and more generally the objects of judgement, were wholly independent from the concerns of psychology. This independence secured the objectivity of logic and mathematics and enabled a distinction between truth and what was thought to be true to be made. The development of accounts of understanding, thinking and meaning something could be assigned to empirical psychology and were no longer a matter for serious philosophical concern. Wittgenstein repudiated Russell's scientific conception of philosophy. On Russell's conception philosophy was continuous with science. Philosophy did not have access to sources of insight unavailable to science and neither did its results differ markedly from those which science could produce. Philosophy was the most general of the sciences and an investigation into the foundations of reality. It diverged from science in its concern with the critical scrutiny of the principles of reasoning in scientific inquiry and in ordinary life. Philosophy described the most general structures of reality. Russell thought that scientific method in philosophy was the method of logical analysis and advances would be made through this. This method would enable philosophy to discard metaphysical systems and instead emulate science by proposing hypotheses which would allow gradual approximations to the truth. Part of the description of the most general features of reality comprised the discovery and cataloguing of logical forms. The method of logical analysis examined the logical forms that were essential for any constructions. Logical form is the structure expressed by logic which reveals those aspects which are relevant to valid argumentation. Russell thought that the meaning of a word is the object which it refers to and that sentences are combinations of names. The logical principles which govern words stem from the objects which they refer to. Each meaningful sentence can be dissolved by analysis into its constituents. The analysis of the meaning of a word corresponds to the logical structure of the object it refers to. Logical analysis thus clarifies both language and the nature of reality. Russell's adherence to this conception of analysis can reasonably be summarized as a commitment to logical atomism. He maintained that logic constituted a logically perfect language which reflected the structure of thought and reality. As the conception of logical analysis developed Russell became aware of the increasing gap between the grammatical and logical forms of sentences. He thought that a lack of precision in natural languages created problems of reference and other difficulties. Logical analysis displayed the underlying logical form of natural language sentences and recognition of such forms would resolve these problems.

In his celebrated theory of definite descriptions Russell aimed to solve a number of puzzles which included accounting for the gap between the grammatical and logical forms of sentences, and Frege's difficulty about sense and reference. Russell distinguished between proper names and descriptions on the grounds that the former had a meaning solely in virtue of what they stood for whilst a description was not a name of any kind. His theory of descriptions in 'On denoting' (Russell, 1956b) provided an account of how the grammatical form of a sentence may hide the actual logical form of the proposition expressed and showed that descriptions have a distinct logical form from that of proper names. For example, in the sentence 'The present king of France is bald', the definite description 'The present king of France' played a role quite different from that of a proper name such as 'Scott' in the sentence 'Scott is bald'. Descriptions were not to be regarded as terms that refer as names do but instead as signs which had no meaning in isolation but were given meaning by contextual definitions that treated the sentences in which they occurred. Descriptions made a systematic contribution to the meanings of the sentences in which they occurred but without expressing propositional content (*Principia Mathematica*, 1910). However, certain kinds of descriptions posed problems. For example, according to the law of the excluded middle, it must be the case that the sentence 'The present king of France is bald' is either true or false. However, either possibility appeared to entail the existence of a present king of France which is clearly not a desirable result. Russell's analysis of a definite description exposed some of its apparent ontological commitments by indicating how the grammatical form of a sentence and the logical form of the proposition it expressed were related. He analysed the grammatical form of the sentence 'The present king of France is bald' as having the logical form of the proposition 'There is an x such that x is king of France, and x is bald, and for all y, if y is king of France, then y is identical to x'. The sentence 'It is not the case that there exists a present king of France who is bald' is true because no such individual as the present king of France exists. It is therefore possible to deny the sentence 'The present king of France is bald' without being committed to the existence of a present King of France. Wittgenstein was interested in Russell's theory of definite descriptions and sought to apply it with modification to fit descriptions of complex objects which were characterized by enumerating their parts. He accepted this method of ensuring that sentences containing definite descriptions have a determinate sense.

A problem with Russell's position about logical analysis was that of explaining how false propositions were possible. A true proposition corresponded to a fact but no fact corresponded to a false proposition even though it was meaningful. Russell adopted the multiple relation theory of judgement according to which judgement was viewed as a multiple relation between an individual, the constituents of the judgement, and their logical form (which is how they are united). This theory of judgement circumvented the difficulty of explaining how a false proposition was possible by maintaining that an individual was acquainted with the constituents of a proposition rather than the proposition as a whole. Wittgenstein criticized this theory on the grounds that it permitted an individual to judge a non-sense as there is no guarantee that the constituents of a proposition are combined in a significant fashion. He developed the picture theory of meaning in the *Tractatus* out of the criticisms of Russell's theory.

PICTURE THEORY OF MEANING

The *Tractatus* was primarily concerned with the logical analysis of language. The picture theory of meaning lay at the core of the book and was a detailed treatment of the prerequisites of symbolic representation in general. Wittgenstein had learnt about the practice of representing traffic accidents in Parisian law courts through using models and this was when the pictorial nature of propositions first occurred to him. Prior to offering an explanation of how propositions represent, the *Tractatus* provided an account of representation in general (2.1–2.225). Wittgenstein remarked that 'We make to ourselves pictures of the facts' (2.1) and 'The picture is a model of reality' (2.12). He thought that the essence of language lies in the representation of how things are. Representation is possible through agreement in form between what represents and what is being represented. Any picture consists of a multiplicity of elements that together constitute the picture. Since a state of affairs is a possible combination of objects (2.01), and each element in a picture represents an object, the combination of objects in a picture represents a state of affairs (2.131). The structure of a picture is how the elements in it must be arranged in order for it to represent how the objects in a state of affairs are combined, and this structure is determined by convention (2.15). By definition a particular structure is possessed by a particular picture. The picture theory of meaning is connected with Wittgenstein's criticisms of Russell's multiple relation theory of judgement. He objected to Russell's theory on the grounds that from the proposition that an individual judges aRb (that is a in the relation R to b) the proposition that aRb or not aRb must follow directly without the employment of any other premises. Wittgenstein's reasoning for this was that if an individual judges truly that aRb then what is judged to be the case is exactly what is the case thus the thought reaches up to reality and does not stop prior to the fact. However, if an individual judges falsely that aRb then what is judged to be the case is exactly what is not the case as what is the case is not aRb. This argument is what motivated Wittgenstein's comment that 'the picture is linked with reality; it reaches up to it' (2.1511). It is useful to observe how minimal Wittgenstein's notion of pictorial form is. The pictorial form needed to represent a certain state of affairs is simply the possibility of arranging the elements of a picture in a way that mirrors the combination of objects in that state of affairs (2.161). What form the arrangement takes will differ for different representations. The pictorial form is the possibility of that arrangement and this ensures that the arrangement has to be shared by the picture and state of affairs (2.15–2.172). Wittgenstein allowed considerable flexibility in what counted as a picture in that a picture could be more or less abstract, contain varying amounts of detail and complexity, and have a greater or lesser resemblance to what it represents. There must be a minimum which is shared between the state of affairs and the picture for the picture even to be an incorrect representation and this minimum is the logical form (2.18). Wittgenstein remarked that if 'the form of representation is the logical form, then the picture is called a logical picture' (2.181) and 'Every picture is *also* a logical picture' (2.182). The *Tractatus* analysed how pictures may be compared with reality (2.201–2.225). Every picture represents a possible state of affairs that may be termed its sense (2.202). Wittgenstein stated that the 'proposition contains the possibility of the states of affairs which it represents' (2.203). A proposition represents a certain state of affairs through the possibility of arranging the elements of the proposition in a way that mirrors the combination of objects in that state of affairs. The picture must make sense independently of whether the possible state of affairs represented agrees with reality (2.22). It follows that a picture represents something even if what it represents does not agree with reality. It is a true picture if the possible state of affairs the picture represents agrees with reality and otherwise it is a false picture (2.222). No picture will itself show whether it is true or false because for this the picture must be compared with reality (2.223f.).

The account of propositional representation (3–4.0641) is an application of the prior account of representation in general (2.1–2.225) and shares the features of representation in general.

Every proposition is a truth-functional combination of elementary propositions and so through the account of elementary propositions the picture theory of meaning is able to explain the basis of propositional representation. The conditions for a proposition having sense rest on the possibility of representation. Wittgenstein remarked that a 'logical picture of facts is the thought' (3). He held that thoughts have an identical structure to the propositions which express them (3.2) but he did not try to explain what constitutes a thought. Only possible states of affairs can be thought of (3.02). In a proposition a thought is expressed in a manner perceptible to the senses (3.1). However, it might be questioned whether a proposition is the sole perceptible expression of a thought as other remarks in the *Tractatus* seem to indicate that various forms of pictorial expression would also be expressions of thoughts. Taking Wittgenstein's view that a picture is a combination of elements the issue of what the elements of a logical picture and a thought are arises. This is one instance of where his commitment to anti-psychologism raised difficulties because it led him to hold that the sort of relationship between the constituents of a logical picture and a thought was not a matter for philosophical investigation but a question for psychology. It is perhaps not surprising given his anti-psychologism that the *Tractatus* provided very little comment about thoughts. However, thoughts are exemplary logical pictures as the logical structure of a thought comprises its entire pictorial form. Clearly logical pictures are dependent upon the laws of logic so a thought is unable to represent anything which contravenes these laws (for the same reasons as a spatial representation that contradicts the laws of geometry cannot be produced) (3.03–3.0321). Thoughts cannot represent logic because a picture (thought) cannot represent its pictorial form (logic) (2.172). The representational form of thought cannot be investigated by thought as a picture is delimited by the representational form it has (2.174). What the representational form of thought is remains a mysterious and ill-defined mental phenomenon.

Wittgenstein claimed that a proposition did not contain the possible state of affairs which it represents since if it did the proposition could not be false (3.13). The reason for this is that if a proposition is true it represents a state of affairs which exists. A proposition is not a complex (3.14ff.). He commented that 'We must not say, "The complex sign '*aRb*' says '*a* stands in relation *R* to *b*' "; but we must say, "*That* '*a*' stands in a certain relation to '*b*' says *that aRb*' '

(3.1432). However, a proposition is composite and does not simply consist of names. Wittgenstein distinguished between names and propositions when he remarked that names resembled points and propositions resembled arrows (3.144). A point of this remark is that if a name does not name something then it is not a meaningful symbol. In contrast a proposition must make sense independently of whether the possible state of affairs represented agrees with reality. Propositions which have sense are bipolar, which is to say that they are either true or false (*NB*, p. 94). (This commitment to bipolarity is part of the realist stance of the *Tractatus*.) There are as many names as objects in a fully analysed proposition (3.2). It is clear that names refer to objects (3.203) but it has been disputed whether they include relations as well. Evidence from Wittgenstein's middle period indicated that he thought that analysis would not cause the names of relations to disappear (*LWL*, p. 120), so it follows that names include relations. Finding examples in natural language of what are regarded as names in the *Tractatus* is difficult. This is because even terms which appear to be singular, such as 'Oxford', will not be regarded as names as further analysis will cause their disappearance. In a proposition it is a matter of convention that a name represents an object and that a certain relation between names represents a certain relation between objects (3.22 and 3.322). Names are signs which cannot be analysed further (3.26) and understanding a name is knowing the object it refers to. Wittgenstein stated that 'Every defined sign signifies *via* those signs by which it is defined, and the definitions show the way' and 'Names *cannot* be taken to pieces by definition (nor any sign which alone and independent has a meaning)' (3.261). The distinction between signs and symbols in the *Tractatus* was complex. However, the fundamental difference was that a sign is a sound or inscription which can be perceived and a symbol is a sign which has been connected to reality. Wittgenstein claimed that if a particular combination of signs did not make sense this would be because this combination was not linked to reality (5.4733). For example, the combination of signs 'Socrates is identical' is nonsense (5.473) since it did not meet the requirement for being a symbol.

Wittgenstein held that the rules of logical syntax constituted an ideal language for the use of signs (3.325). The use of the term 'syntax' reflected the fact that logical syntax was solely concerned with the syntax of sign combinations and had no stipulations about semantics or the types of object a symbol could refer to (3.33). An essential feature was that the same sign must not have more than one meaning. Wittgenstein applied his restriction that only syntactic considerations featured in the rules of logical syntax to criticize Russell's theory of types. He argued that a problem with the theory of types was that the formulation of its syntactic rules invoked considerations about the types of object a symbol could refer to and that this must be avoided (3.331). It was not possible to say that an entity was of a certain type, such as X being an individual rather than a set, but this could be shown by the symbol used. Wittgenstein maintained that what the theory of types had attempted to demonstrate could be shown by the employment of symbols (3.332f.). The rules of logical syntax were governed by logic so its syntax was logical rather than being that of natural language. These rules were both comprehensive and determinate. They demarcated the bounds of sense by unequivocally fixing whether and what sense any possible combination of signs made (5.4541). The rules of logical syntax were related to the important distinction between the notions of nonsense and senseless. Nonsensical propositions violated the rules of logical syntax. Logical analysis demonstrated that these propositions break logical syntax rules (3.323f.). Senseless propositions do not say anything. Tautologies and contradictions are senseless (4.461) and thus have a unique position in relation to other propositions. The *Tractatus* claimed that all symbol systems including natural languages must conform to the rules of logical syntax. A consequence of this is that language was regarded as being akin to a formal system and treated from the perspective of being a calculus. The conjunction of a logical and syntactic system of formation and transformation rules with assignments of meaning to names together fix the meaning of every grammatical (that is, well-formed) sentence in the language. Taken together with appropriate facts this calculus of meaning unequivocally determines the truth value of each sentence. Wittgenstein thought that the rules of logical syntax govern natural language even though speakers are unaware of them. The grammar of a natural language hid the complex system of rules which underpinned it and these rules could be exposed by logical analysis. The grammatical forms of sentences may disguise the actual logical form of the proposition expressed but the rules of logical syntax would display this logical form.

Wittgenstein offered his own version of the context principle that a word only has a meaning in the context of sentence. He remarked that 'Only the proposition has sense; only in the context of a proposition has a name meaning' (3.3). This comment embodied the claims that only a proposition had sense and that names were meaningless outside of propositional contexts. The combination of these claims suggests that Wittgenstein sought to invoke the context principle as a reason for refusing to attribute meaning to expressions which are not propositions. However, it remains unclear just how this principle would support such a refusal. In passing it is worth observing that he gave another version of the context principle which cited elementary propositions. This was that 'The name occurs in the proposition only in the context of the elementary proposition' (4.23). The sense of a proposition was a function of the meaning of the names which constituted it (3.326). Only in the context of a proposition was the function of a name that of contributing to the determination of the truth conditions of that proposition (3.327). Wittgenstein differentiated between the contingent and necessary features of a proposition as every one has both. The contingent features stemmed from the particular conventions of the language in which it was stated whilst the necessary features were those which were essential for expressing its sense (3.34). The combinatorial possibilities of names had to mirror those of objects. The correlation of a name with an object determined the combinatorial possibilities for that name (3.334). In the *Tractatus* logical space was the collection of logical possibilities. A point in logical space was fixed by an elementary proposition (3.4ff.).

Wittgenstein sometimes commented that a proposition was really a thought (3.5–4). For example, he stated 'The thought is the significant proposition' (4). There seems to be some tension between this standpoint and the view expressed earlier in the book that a proposition was the expression of a thought (3.2). The pictorial nature of propositions clearly emerged in his remark that a 'proposition is a picture' (4.01). Propositions served as models (4.01) and constructed reality (4.023). The representational character of propositions was based on the rules of logical syntax (4.011ff.). A proposition was a picture of reality which represented the state of affairs it described (4.016–4.021). Wittgenstein commented that ' "A proposition shows its sense", that is, "how things stand *if* it is true. And it *says that* they do so stand" ' (4.022). It was pivotal to the picture theory of meaning that if a proposition was true it represented a state of affairs which existed once its elements had been correlated with objects. This correlation consisted of a method of projection. A proposition represented a possible state of affairs and its sense was determinate. No proposition will itself show whether it is true or false because for this the proposition must be compared with reality (2.223 and 4.05). If a proposition was true it represented a state of affairs which existed. This position about representation allowed Wittgenstein to explain how it was possible for a proposition to be false. A false proposition represented a state of affairs which did not exist. Wittgenstein raised questions about the creativity of language, such as how it was possible to understand sentences which have not been heard previously (4.02 and 4.027). The solution which he offered to these problems rested upon the picture theory. It is a matter of convention that a name represented an object and that a certain relation between names represented a certain relation between objects. The correlation of a name with an object determined the combinatorial possibilities for that name. These were the only conventions which were required for a certain relation between names to mean a certain relation between objects and indeed sufficient for the proposition to represent the situation (4.024). Given this the creativity of language was possible as the rules of logical syntax could be applied to a finite collection of names to produce elementary propositions. In turn the truth-functional combination of elementary propositions could create infinitely many propositions. These combinatorial possibilities accounted for how it was possible to understand sentences which have not been heard previously whilst every new name which a speaker encountered required an explanation (4.026). Wittgenstein further developed his conception of the pictorial aspects of a proposition when he claimed that a proposition was a logical picture but not a pure one (4.03). The pictorial character of a proposition was comprised by its structural connection to the state of affairs it represented. This illuminates Wittgenstein's remark that 'In a proposition a situation is, as it were, assembled by way of experiment' (4.031). He was claiming that a proposition put together a state of affairs which was then tested against reality (thus the idea of experiment) to see if it matched. Logical analysis indicated that propositions were pictorial in the sense that a proposition had to have an identical number of distinct elements to the state of affairs it represented (4.04). A consequence of this is that for a proposition to represent there had to be a one to one correlation between its names and the objects in the state of affairs it represented.

LIMITS OF LANGUAGE AND PHILOSOPHY

Wittgenstein's critique of language sought to differentiate sense from nonsense or alternatively put to demarcate the limits of sense. It was not possible to describe the limits of sense because there was nothing which lay beyond the boundaries of sense to be characterized. If these limits could be articulated then the negation of their articulation would constitute sense but if it did then the articulation would not be characterizing the limits of sense. Wittgenstein asserted that 'What *can* be shown *cannot* be said' (4.1212). The distinction between saying and showing relates to the bounds of sense since although they cannot be described they can be shown. The distinction between saying and showing is important to both the assertions about language and logic, and about value in the *Tractatus*. Indeed some commentators have argued that the distinction holds these two parts of the book together by proscribing propositions about the fundamental features of general symbolic representation and certain kinds of pronouncements concerning value. Wittgenstein argued that particular sorts of claims about language and logic which propositions aimed to make were actually shown by bipolar propositions. One significant group of propositions attempted to state the logical form which was shared by propositions and what they represented (or as it is sometimes put the inexpressible harmony between thought and reality) although this could only be shown. For example, Wittgenstein commented that 'The propositions *show* the logical form of reality. They exhibit it' (4.121). Other propositions of this sort included the shared pictorial form of a picture and what is represented (2.172–2.174), that a proposition showed its sense (4.022), that logical constants did not represent and that the logic of the facts could not be represented (4.0312), that a proposition and reality had the same number of distinct elements (4.041), and that a proposition was about a particular object (4.1211 and 5.535). Another group was what propositions sought to articulate about the meaning of signs and the sense of propositions. Propositions about the meaning of signs (3.33ff.) and that two signs have an identical meaning (6.23) could not be stated but could be shown. A further group was what propositions attempted to say about the logical relations between them as once again this could only be shown. These included propositions concerned with logical propositions being tautologies and not referring to logical constants (4.0621 and 4.461) and about one proposition following from another (5.12–5.132).

The idea that formal concepts were not genuine concepts had significant links to the difference between saying and showing. Wittgenstein distinguished between formal and genuine concepts (4.126–4.1274). If it could be said what the content of a concept was then it was a genuine one. If its content could not be stated and it was a category of concept then it was a formal concept. Wittgenstein asserted 'That anything falls under a formal concept as an object belonging to it, cannot be expressed by a proposition. But it is shown in the symbol for the object itself' (4.126). He was arguing that the sign showed which formal concept an entity came under. For example, the numerical sign showed that the entity signified a number and fell under the formal concept of number. Wittgenstein remarked the sign which signified the 'characteristics of a formal concept is, therefore, a characteristic feature of all symbols, whose meanings fall under the concept. The expression of a formal concept is therefore a propositional variable in which only this characteristic feature is constant' (4.126). A formal concept was characterized by a variable and the value which the variable had, such as being a number, indicated the things which fell under this concept (4.126f.). What propositions employing formal concepts tried to say was actually shown by ordinary propositions whose constituent words belonged to the formal concept which was designated by a given variable. For example, what propositions about numbers attempted to say was shown by ordinary propositions containing a numerical variable. Propositions such as 'The number two can move to Mars' are nonsense and show the conceptual points that numbers do not have spatial locations and so on. Wittgenstein thought that every thing had a formal concept which it came under (4.12721). Commentators are divided about what formal concepts there are. This issue cannot be settled because no precise evidence about what formal concepts comprise was given and there was no indication that the list of them was supposed to be exhaustive (4.126 and 4.1272). Probably the most that can be done is to surmise what formal concepts Wittgenstein might have placed upon the list by working with the named ones such as complex (4.1272). For example, it might be argued that the notion of 'combination' is a formal concept because it could be given a role in the definition of complex.

A major group of propositions which attempted to say that which could only be shown were those that tried to articulate the structure of thought and reality. The *Tractatus* drew 'a limit to thinking, or rather – not to thinking, but to the expression of thoughts' and the 'limit can, therefore, only be drawn in language and what lies on the other side of the limit will be simply nonsense' (Preface). Wittgenstein considered the idea of the limits of language (5.5561, 5.6f. and 6.124). He commented that *'The limits of my language* mean the limits of my world' (5.6). Since representations in language mirror the reality they represent the limits of language delineate the limits of the reality. Only what is in reality can be represented and anything which lies beyond this including the limits of reality itself cannot. If this was possible it would mean that language has exceeded its limits. Solipsism lay on the boundary between the assertions about language and logic, and about value in the *Tractatus*. Wittgenstein remarked that 'In fact what solipsism *means*, is quite correct, only it cannot be *said*, but shows itself' (5.62). He acquired his interest in solipsism from Schopenhauer. For example, the latter's 'The world is my idea' from *The World as Will and Representation* was reflected in remarks such as 'That the world is *my* world, shows itself in the fact that the limits of the language (*the* language which I understand) mean the limits of *my* world' (5.62). The subject of experience lay at the limits of reality as he stated that 'The subject does not belong to the world but it is a limit of the world' (5.632). Some commentators, such as Pears, perceive solipsism as the dominant theme of the *Tractatus* but this is a minority opinion.

A final group of propositions which attempted to say that which could only be shown were those that tried to articulate the inexpressibility of value. Propositions of this sort included that there are laws of nature (6.36), the ethical plus everything 'higher' (6.42f.), and the philosophical propositions of the *Tractatus* itself (6.54). The distinction between saying and showing was relevant to Wittgenstein's conception of the status of philosophical propositions. He argued that philosophy must only say what can be said. Philosophy will not propose philosophical propositions as these are nonsensical because they attempt to say what can only be shown. For example, these propositions employ formal concepts.

Frege and Russell maintained that logic constituted a logically perfect language which reflected the structure of thought and reality. They held that natural languages were logically defective because they did not satisfy this requirement about reflection. Wittgenstein disagreed with their view that natural language was logically defective as it was able to express every sense (4.002). However, he thought that natural language was a potential source of confusion because it 'disguises the thought' (4.002) in hiding logical form. Logical analysis was to be used to calculate and exhibit logical form. Wittgenstein claimed that a logically perfect language that apparently had expressive capacities which were not present in natural language was not required. He held that the rules of logical syntax constituted an ideal language for the use of signs (3.325). Wittgenstein expressed a significant aspect of his conception of philosophy when he remarked that (4.003):

> Most propositions and questions, that have been written about philosophical matters are not false but nonsensical. We cannot, therefore, answer questions of this kind at all, but only state their nonsensicality. Most propositions and questions of the philosophers result from the fact that we do not understand the logic of our language.

Philosophical problems were not dissolved by the creation of theories as such theories were really attempts to answer questions which are not genuine ones or to resolve problems which were spurious. Philosophy clarified meaningful propositions with the result being not a gain in knowledge but the removal of confusion. Philosophical difficulties arose from failure to comprehend language properly. A key conception is that all philosophy is a critique of language. Philosophical problems should be resolved by logical analysis as this clearly exhibited the logical features of language. Wittgenstein held that a philosophical investigation examined the relationship between natural language and logical syntax because the gap between the two is the origin of philosophical difficulties. Wittgenstein in reference to Russell's theory of definite descriptions commented approvingly that 'Russell's merit is to have shown that the apparent logical form of the proposition need not be its real form' (4.0031). The philosophical methodology of logical analysis eliminated philosophical perplexity by showing that philosophical theories, such as those of metaphysics, were characteristically nonsense rather than false as they had contravened the rules of logical syntax (4.002ff.).

Wittgenstein disagreed with philosophers, such as Russell, who conceived of philosophy as the most general science. For Russell scientific method would enable philosophy to discard metaphysical systems and instead emulate science by proposing hypotheses which would allow gradual approximations to the truth. Wittgenstein did not think that philosophy was a kind of science which aimed at developing theories and discovering new facts. He stated that 'the word "philosophy" must mean something which stands above or below, but not beside the natural sciences' (4.111) and that philosophy 'limits the disputable sphere of natural science' (4.113). Wittgenstein claimed that the totality of true propositions was identical with the body of the natural sciences (4.11). However, his position raised the question of what place disciplines, such as history and social science, had. At first appearance an implication of his view is that they did not consist of true propositions. Wittgenstein shared Frege and Russell's commitment to anti-psychologism and claimed that philosophy had no closer connections to psychology than to any other natural science (4.1121). However, Wittgenstein and Russell differed about whether discovery was possible in philosophy and one example of their divergent attitudes to this was over the possibility of discovering logical forms. Wittgenstein was clear that philosophy was an activity whose objective was the logical clarification of thoughts and that a work in philosophy essentially consisted of elucidations (4.112). He claimed that philosophy 'should limit the unthinkable from within through the thinkable' (4.114). The aim of philosophy was the achievement of a correct logical point of view (4.1213) and this involved an understanding of what could be said and its limits. Wittgenstein thought that the task of philosophy could be definitively completed and that he had done this in the *Tractatus*.

CHAPTER 3

METAPHYSICS OF THE *TRACTATUS*

CONNECTING LANGUAGE AND REALITY

Russell's logical atomism was most clearly presented in his 'The philosophy of logical atomism' (1918) which he stated was 'very largely concerned with explaining certain ideas which I learnt from my friend and former pupil Ludwig Wittgenstein' (Russell 1956c, p. 177). He favoured the expression logical atomism because the atoms that constitute the world were to be discovered by logical analysis (ibid., p. 179). Partly as a result of Russell's description the term logical atomism subsequently became associated with the *Tractatus* although Wittgenstein himself did not use it. The majority of interpretations regard the book as espousing realism although it should be noted that some more linguistically oriented interpretations give conceptual priority to the symbolism.

The very start of the *Tractatus* contained a series of pronouncements about the world which logically follow from those about language but this relationship is concealed by their position in the work. These remarks argued for the conception that representations in language are isomorphic with the world that they represent and in doing so manifest a commitment to realism. The abstract generalization which pervaded the book is evident from its opening. 'The world is everything that is the case' (1) could be understood in the light of what follows as claiming that the world is everything that is represented by the totality of true propositions. 'The world is the totality of facts, not of things' (1.1) argued that the world consisted of facts rather espousing the traditional atomistic conception that reality was comprised of objects. Wittgenstein did not provide any examples of either facts or objects. 'What is the case, the fact, is the existence of states of affairs' (2) asserted that existing states of affairs[1] constituted the whole of reality. 'A state of affairs is a combination of objects (entities, things)' (2.01) meant that various configurations of objects made up states of affairs. A state of affairs is either existent or possible. It is fundamental to the nature of an object that it occurs in combination with other objects in states of affairs (2.0123). The character of reality was constrained by the objects because all possible states of affairs were configurations of them (2.0124).

The objects of the *Tractatus* raise a number of questions. The claim that objects are simple (2.02) is that they are wholly devoid of complexity. In the book Wittgenstein provided no guidance about how to identify an object. The issue of whether and in what ways he thought that such objects could be recognized is complex. Evidence from the *Notebooks 1914–1916* suggests Wittgenstein held that it was possible in principle to specify objects provided logical analysis was carried far enough. For example, he observed that it seemed to him 'perfectly possible that patches in our visual field are simple objects, in that we do not perceive any single point of a patch separately; the visual appearances of stars even seem certainly to be so' (*NB*, p. 64) Here 'patches in our visual field' mean sections of the visual field with no noticeable parts. The claim here was that certain entities would either count as objects or would turn out to do so. In the *Tractatus*, Wittgenstein had not resolved these questions or decided upon what would be regarded as an instance of a simple object. Later he remarked that at the time his thought had 'been that he was a *logician*; and that it was not his business, as a logician, to try to decide whether this thing or that was a simple thing or a complex thing, that being a purely *empirical* matter!' (Malcolm 1984, p. 70). It seems evident that Wittgenstein's anti-psychologism which sought to ensure that generally the objects of judgement were wholly independent from the concerns of psychology was a major contributory factor in his inability to identify the objects of the *Tractatus*. Arguably, he thought that the sort of analysis required to determine what they were more properly came under the province of psychology.

The ultimate constituents of reality were to be revealed by a process of logical analysis. 'Every statement about complexes can be analysed into a statement about their constituent parts, and into those propositions which completely describe the complexes' (2.0201) argued that any complex consisted of simpler parts. From the previous remark it followed that these parts were objects. Remarks (2.021–2.0211) comprised part of the argument which asserted the existence of objects. Wittgenstein remarked that 'Objects form the substance of the world. Therefore they cannot be compound' (2.021) and 'If the world had no substance, then whether a proposition had sense would depend on whether another proposition was true' (2.0211). He stressed that an essential prerequisite for the determinacy of sense was that objects must be simple both epistemologically and metaphysically. Wittgenstein maintained that his view that 'It would then be impossible to form a picture of the world (true or false)' (2.0212) followed from his position that if the world lacked substance then whether a proposition had sense would depend on the truth of another proposition (2.0211). Objects were what any possible world had in common with the real world (2.022) and accordingly they constituted the world's 'fixed form' (2.022f.). The point is that objects could not be created or destroyed since any possible world must contain exactly the same objects as the real world. Indeed change of any kind was simply an alteration in their combination. Wittgenstein commented that material properties 'are first presented by the propositions – first formed by the configurations of the objects' (2.0231). This suggests that what expressed a property was the way objects were combined. An object's internal properties determined the possibilities of its combination with other objects and this was its logical form (2.0233). The claim that 'objects form the substance of the world' (2.021), taken in conjunction with the view that 'substance is what exists independently of what is the case' (2.024), amounted to the assertion that objects existed. Objects were the content of states of affairs whose form was the way in which their constituent objects were combined. It followed that the totality of objects was both 'form and content' (2.025). Wittgenstein stated that 'The object is the fixed, the existent; the configuration is the changing, the variable' (2.0271). Once again he emphasized that objects could not be changed and persisted but their combinations alter and lack stability. Wittgenstein argued that 'In the state of affairs objects hang one in another, like the links of a chain' (2.03). The reason for the chain metaphor was that objects combined into states of affairs in which they stood in a determinate relationship to each other (with each one as a link in the chain). The idea was that each object played an equal role in securing the unity of the states of affairs in which it occurred and by extension each name played an equal role in securing the unity of the proposition in which it occurred. How objects were connected was the structure of a state of affairs (2.032). The form which a state of affairs had was its structural possibilities (2.033).

Wittgenstein thought that every proposition had a complete analysis and that in a wholly analysed proposition there were the same number of names as objects (3.2). Some of the unclarity in the conception of analysis was created because Wittgenstein rejected any ontology of unclear entities expressed by sentences. Analysis was the replacement of apparent names with terms for complexes with the same reference together with eliminative paraphrase of the latter. It was presupposed that there was knowledge both of the correct analyses of apparent names and of the contextual definitions by means of which terms for complexes were eliminated. It followed that the endpoint of analysis will contain no terms for complexes. Whenever an apparent name occurred that appeared to mention a complex this was only because it was not a genuine name. Objects were to be discovered by understanding fully analysed propositions. The conception of analysis presented in the book made it evident why Wittgenstein thought that analysis should terminate in this way. An unanalysed proposition derived its sense from its analysis and therefore if a proposition had an analysis which never ended it would never acquire a sense. Wittgenstein remarked 'That a propositional element signifies a complex can be seen from an indeterminateness in the propositions in which it occurs. We *know* that everything is not yet determined by this proposition' (3.24). He thought that if simple signs stood for complex objects the propositions which the signs occurred in would have indeterminate sense. An indeterminate sense in a proposition was supposed to have the role of being a sign of further analysability. However, it does not follow that the absence of an indeterminate sense indicates that a proposition has been fully analysed. Even with further justification for the claim that the absence of an indeterminate sense indicated that a proposition had been fully analysed, there is still the difficulty that it is not clear what is meant by an indeterminate sense in a proposition. The failure to supply an adequate explanation of how to recognize when a proposition was fully analysed had the consequence that a satisfactory account of how an object could be identified as such could not be produced. Every proposition had a unique final analysis which revealed it to be a truth-function of elementary propositions which asserted the existence of states of affairs (3.25, 4.21, 4.221 and 5).

Wittgenstein commented that 'It is obvious that in the analysis of propositions we must come to elementary propositions, which consist of names in immediate combination' (4.221). He thought that a fully analysed proposition consisted exclusively of genuine names in immediate combination which referred to objects and that there would be no other referring expressions. A proposition 'reaches through the whole logical space' (3.42), which meant that it had a truth value with respect to every possible world.

Elementary propositions formed the basis of all linguistic representation and hence the foundation of the picture theory of meaning. The claim that elementary propositions were logically independent of each other was a key element of the *Tractatus*. The existence of a logical dependency between propositions was taken to be a mark of internal complexity. No two elementary propositions can either be inconsistent with or entail each other. If 'p' entails 'q' its sense contains that of 'q' which is to say that analysis has to reveal 'q' to be one of the truth-functional components of 'p'. By the same token if 'p' contradicts 'q' it entailed and thereby contained its negation. In both cases 'p' is complex and not elementary (4.1211, 4.211 and 5.134). This requirement about the logical independence of propositions was supported by Wittgenstein's view that propositions were truth-functions of elementary ones as this assumed that an elementary proposition could be ascribed a truth value independently of all other propositions. He thought that when all complexity was eliminated by analysis the elementary propositions which resulted from this were logically independent. Each elementary proposition could be true or false independently of the truth or falsity of the others (4.211) and thus they were logically independent. Their logical independence implies that if 'p' is elementary its negation could not be as the two are contradictories. Elementary propositions could not be inferred from one another (5.134). A false elementary proposition is not the negation of a true one instead it represents a different combination of objects which did not exist (2.06 and 4.022). Elementary propositions represent states of affairs which is to say that they assert the existence of a certain combination of objects. If they are true then that state of affairs exists (4.21). This implied that all elementary propositions represented either truly or falsely the existence of a state of affairs. These propositions stated that something was the case and that objects stood in a certain way (4.021–4.023). Elementary propositions were concatenations of names for objects (4.22). These propositions represented states of affairs by combining the names in a way which corresponded to a possible combination of objects (4.22f.). The idea of simple objects required that elementary propositions must represent definite combinations of objects which could not be destroyed. Propositions about complexes could be false either if the complex did not exist or if it lacked the property ascribed to it. In contrast, an elementary proposition ruled out this possibility because the objects referred to by its names must be arranged in a way that mirrored how the names stood in the proposition (4.25f.). The general problem of the manifest incompatibility of apparently unanalysable statements poses a difficulty for Wittgenstein's view that elementary propositions are logically independent. One particular form it takes is the colour exclusion problem. This can be expressed as the idea that two colours cannot simultaneously be at one place in an individual's visual field and the force of this lies in the fact that this exclusion is not prima facie logically impossible. It should be observed that this problem has implications for the treatment of logical necessity in the *Tractatus*.

Formal logic can have quite different philosophical interpretations, such as in the treatment of quantifiers. Wittgenstein took formal logic from Frege and Russell but offered differing philosophical interpretations of certain aspects of it. Logic provided the structure of what could be said. He inherited the idea from Frege and Russell that propositions are composed of function and argument (3.318 and 5.47). Wittgenstein remarked that 'Propositions are truth-functions of elementary propositions. (An elementary proposition is a truth-function of itself)' (5). He thought that every proposition is a truth-functional combination of elementary propositions. Wittgenstein supplied the first presentation of Frege's logic in the form of what has become known as truth tables. Truth-functional combinations of propositions had two limiting cases, namely those of tautology and contradiction. Tautologies and contradictions are termed senseless (which means that they do not say anything) (4.461) but they are not nonsensical (4.4611). Tautologies and contradictions did not represent reality because 'for the one allows *every* possible state of affairs, the other *none*' (4.462). The characterization of senseless was relevant to the status of the propositions of logic as Wittgenstein remarked that 'But all propositions of logic say the same thing. That is, nothing' (5.43). The propositions of logic, such as the laws of inference (5.132), were senseless.

Wittgenstein followed Frege in allocating a fundamental role in logic to the propositional connectives 'if . . . then', 'not', 'and', 'or', the quantifiers, and the sign of identity. He termed these 'the logical constants' and the *Tractatus* devoted significant attention to their operation. Wittgenstein differed from Frege and Russell in his denial that quantifiers are logical constants. He thought they failed to do justice to the fact that the understanding of universally and existentially quantified propositions presupposed an understanding of elementary propositions. This was because the sense of universally quantified and existentially quantified propositions was a function of certain elementary propositions and thus had to be explained by reference to them (4.411 and 5.521). Wittgenstein claimed that universally and existentially quantified propositions were to be analysed away as truth-functions of elementary propositions in accordance with his general principles (5.52–5.523). Universally quantified propositions were treated as equivalent to a possibly infinite conjunction of propositions. Existentially quantified propositions were treated as equivalent to a possibly infinite disjunction of propositions. Unlike Frege and Russell, Wittgenstein sought to do without the concept of identity. He excluded the notion of identity from logical syntax and indicated in various ways how it was possible to eliminate it. He used the identity of the sign which represented an object to express identity and did not employ the identity sign (5.53). The version of Russell's theory of definite descriptions in the *Tractatus* removed the sign for identity (5.532–5.5321). Wittgenstein offered equivalent formulations of Russell's notions which did not invoke identity. He clearly rejected analysis that made use of the identity sign in such a way that it could not be eliminated (5.534). Wittgenstein thought that propositions which employed the identity sign in this fashion were not genuine ones as they sought to say what could only be shown. It was not possible to specify the possible forms of elementary propositions *a priori* (5.553–5.5541 and 5.5571) and these forms were determined by the application of logic (5.557). There could be no resemblance between the apparent forms of propositions which were not elementary and the forms of elementary propositions. Wittgenstein stated that 'There cannot be a hierarchy of the forms of the elementary propositions. Only that which we ourselves construct can we foresee' (5.556). One of the points of this remark was that elementary propositions could not be ordered in the way that non-elementary propositions could be.

The *Tractatus* constructed a systematic edifice using logic which resulted in the general form of the proposition. Wittgenstein commented that 'The general form of proposition is: Such and such is the case' (4.5). This form corresponded to the formal concept of proposition and the range of values it encompassed was the totality of propositions. The bipolarity of propositions permits the composition of more complex propositions from elementary ones (5.441 and 5.47). What all propositions had in common with each other was the only logical constant. Wittgenstein remarked that 'To give the essence of proposition means to give the essence of all description, and therefore the essence of the world' (5.4711). The general propositional form (4.5) was equated with the general form of a truth-function. He stated that 'The general form of truth-function is: $(\rho, \xi, N(\xi))$' (6). ρ represented a list of all elementary propositions. A propositional variable (ξ) and an operation $N(\xi)$ were employed to represent the claim that 'every proposition is the result of successive applications' of this operation to elementary propositions (6.001).

PSEUDO-PROPOSITIONS

A consequence of Wittgenstein's views in the *Tractatus* was that a considerable number of sentences expressed propositions which logical analysis demonstrated to be nonsense. He thought that the propositions of logic, mathematics, the theory of natural science, ethics, aesthetics and philosophy were not genuine ones. That is to say they were pseudo-propositions. The propositions of logic were senseless (6.1). Wittgenstein remarked that 'there can *never* be surprises in logic' (6.1251), which was an expression of his more general view that there were no discoveries to be made in philosophy. He argued that logical theorems do not need to be derived from logical axioms because these theories are tautologies. Their truth can be recognized solely from their symbols and by the calculation of their logical properties. It follows that there was no need to compare them with reality or derive them from other propositions in order to discern their truth (6.113 and 6.126). This challenged the conception of logic that logic consisted of axioms and rules of inference from which theorems could be derived. In turn this undermined the logicist position that mathematics could be securely grounded by deriving it from logic.

Wittgenstein argued that in ordinary life mathematical propositions were only employed in moving from one non-mathematical proposition to another (6.211). He thought that the propositions of mathematics were equations and were thus not genuine ones (6.2). Wittgenstein's reasoning for this view was that in an equation signs on either side of the equals sign can be substituted for one another but if this substitution is possible it must be manifest in the expressions themselves. The fact that signs in equations can be substituted for one another cannot be asserted by a meaningful proposition and must be seen from the expressions themselves (6.232). It follows that equations attempted to say what they showed (6.23) and were therefore pseudo-propositions. Wittgenstein commented 'that the propositions of mathematics can be proved means nothing else than that their correctness can be seen without our having to compare what they express with the facts as regards correctness' (6.2321). He thought that the essential mathematical method was working with equations (6.2341). The *Tractatus* criticized the logicist definition of numbers and submitted a constructive alternative according to which the natural numbers represented stages in the execution of a logical operation. Any sentence containing a numeral could be translated into a sentence representing the application of an operation. An equation like '$2 \times 2 = 4$' can be written as '$\Omega^2, \Omega^2, \times = \Omega^4, \times$'. The repetition of a twofold application of an operation twice is equivalent to its fourfold application (6.241).

The natural sciences mostly consisted of genuine propositions. Science was the 'totality of true propositions' (4.11) and the remarks (6.3ff.) were concerned with the nature of scientific theory. There were general scientific laws of an *a priori* character which were insights into the formulations that genuine propositions about science can take (6.32). It is worth noticing that Wittgenstein regarded the law of induction as a genuine proposition since it was conceivable that it could be false. This is because the occurrence of an event never necessitated the occurrence of another (6.31 and 6.363–6.36311). Natural laws did not describe necessities in the world since the only necessity was logical necessity (6.37) and the only impossibility was logical impossibility (6.375). Wittgenstein then considered an objection to his views about necessity in the form of what is frequently termed the colour exclusion problem and treated the difficulty this posed as merely apparent. He stated that (6.3751):

For two colours, *e.g.* to be at one place in the visual field, is impossible, logically impossible, for it is excluded by the logical structure of colour. Let us consider how this contradiction presents itself in physics. Somewhat as follows: That a particle cannot at the same time have two velocities, *i.e.* that at the same time it cannot be in two places, *i.e.* that particles in different places at the same time cannot be identical.

The analysis described here actually failed to reveal a logical incompatibility between the two statements in question. This is because even granting the correctness of the proposed reduction of the phenomenology of colour perception to facts about the velocities of particles, the fact that the same particle cannot be in two places at the same time still appears to strongly resemble a synthetic *a priori* truth. Wittgenstein was well aware that he had not developed the analysis sufficiently to produce a logical contradiction, but at the time he was confident that in such cases further analysis would always succeed in revealing the incompatibility as logical in character (*NB*, p. 81). He subsequently thought that his attitude was mistaken (see Chapter 4).

Wittgenstein discussed ethics and aesthetics together. He remarked that 'All propositions are of equal value' (6.4). No proposition could express the meaning of the world because all propositions were contingent. Value was not to be found in the world and if there was any genuine value the value of this could not be a contingent matter (6.41). The propositions of ethics and aesthetics could not be said (6.421). Wittgenstein acquired his interest in the ethical nature of the relation between the will and world from Schopenhauer. He thought that the 'will as the subject of the ethical' could not be spoken about (6.423). A good will is its own reward since it accepts whatever occurs with equanimity (6.43). Wittgenstein claimed that there was a mystical attitude which marvelled at the existence of the world (6.45). The problems of life could not be answered and their solution lay in the disappearance of the problem (6.52f.). The *Tractatus* definitely did not appear to be primarily concerned with ethics but a minority of commentators have claimed that it should be interpreted as an ethical work. This interpretation is developed from a conjectured discrepancy between the linguistic, logical and metaphysical constructions which dominate the book, and several remarks in which Wittgenstein suggested that what cannot be said was the most significant part of the book. It is argued that his comment 'the value of this work secondly consists in the fact that it shows how little has been done when these problems have been solved' (Preface) supports this view. Another frequently quoted piece of evidence is that from a letter to Ludwig von Ficker around October–November 1919:

> [this] work consists of two parts: of the one which is here, and of everything which I have *not* written. And precisely this second part is the important one. For the Ethical is delimited from within, as it were, by my book . . . All of that which *many* are *babbling* today, I have defined in my book by remaining silent about it . . .

Against this proposed ethical interpretation of the *Tractatus* it can be observed that these passages are very few in number and all of them may be regarded as external to the contents of the book.

Wittgenstein had a clear Kantian anti-sceptical strategy which dealt with scepticism by considering the bounds of sense (6.51). He thought that philosophical propositions were not genuine ones. He remarked that (6.53):

> The right method of philosophy would be this. To say nothing except what can be said, *i.e.* the propositions of natural science . . . and then always, when someone else wished to say something metaphysical, to demonstrate to him that he had given no meaning to certain signs in his propositions.

If a philosophical proposition was proffered the correct response was to show that it had violated the bounds of sense because it contained signs which had no meaning. Wittgenstein developed this idea when he commented that 'My propositions are elucidatory in this way: he who understands me finally recognises them as nonsensical, when he has climbed out through them, on them, over them' (6.54). Philosophical propositions were nonsense because they attempted to say what could only be shown and thus the *Tractatus* had exceeded its own limits. The concern that the book might potentially be regarded as nonsensical was addressed in the metaphor of the ladder. It was employed to indicate that the work was to be used to 'see the world rightly' (6.54) but subsequently it had to be recognized as nonsense and discarded. Wittgenstein's famous aphorism that 'Whereof one cannot speak, thereof one must be silent' (7) expressed his view that only what can be said should be. New Wittgensteinian interpreters criticize orthodox claims about nonsense in the *Tractatus*. These commentators argue that Wittgenstein's claim that the propositions in the book are nonsensical must be taken seriously and therefore it is mistaken to look for any metaphysical claims in it. Since nonsense is just that, if these propositions are nonsensical then they cannot advocate any metaphysical theories, such as the picture theory of meaning. It does not necessarily follow from this position that there is no value in the contents of the *Tractatus* as Wittgenstein's aim seems to have been to expose as nonsense views which philosophers are tempted to propose. His view that the work must be discarded (6.54) is adduced in support of this. What cannot be said is indicated by the book and furthermore the book itself is part of the inexpressible. Advocates of this interpretation consider how it can be recognized that the book has this status and what its possible significance might be.

THE EARLY AND LATER WORK

Wittgenstein is generally considered to have changed his thinking considerably over the course of his writings. He was acutely aware of the contrast between his early and later periods. Wittgenstein stated that the *Tractatus* and the new thoughts of the *Investigations* should be published together as 'the latter could be seen in the right light only by contrast with and against the background of my old way of thinking' (*Investigations*, Preface, second page). Indeed in 1943 he had proposed to Cambridge University Press that they publish both books together but despite his offer being accepted the plan never materialized. It is not in doubt that there are substantial continuities and discontinuities between the early and the later work as many of the same problems are attacked and previously advocated positions are criticized. Subsequently Wittgenstein rejected what he saw as the dogmatism of his early work. What is controversial is whether there is fundamental continuity or whether the later writings constitute a radical break from the earlier ones. Orthodox interpretations claim a clear break between the early and the later work even when ascertaining some developmental continuity between them. New Wittgensteinian interpretations challenge the orthodox interpretations by emphasizing that the fundamental therapeutic motivation found in the later Wittgenstein should also be attributed to the early. This interpretation argues that the *Tractatus* rejects itself by claiming that its propositions are nonsensical and therefore criticism of this book in the later work does not prove a discontinuity in Wittgenstein's thinking.

Wittgenstein's view of the nature of philosophy had important continuities. From the *Tractatus* onwards, he disagreed with philosophers, such as Russell, who conceived of philosophy as the most general science. Wittgenstein did not think that philosophy was a kind of science which aimed at developing theories and discovering new facts. Philosophical problems were not dissolved by the creation of theories as such theories were really attempts to answer questions which are not genuine ones or to resolve problems which were spurious ones. Philosophy clarified meaningful propositions with the result being not a gain in knowledge but the removal of confusion. Philosophical difficulties arose from failure to comprehend language properly. A key conception is that all philosophy is a critique of language. Philosophical problems should be resolved by logical analysis as this clearly exhibited the logical features of language. Wittgenstein held that a philosophical investigation examined the relationship between natural language and logical syntax because the gap between the two is the origin of philosophical difficulties. The philosophical methodology of logical analysis eliminated philosophical perplexity by showing that philosophical theories, such as those of metaphysics, were characteristically nonsense rather than false as they had contravened the rules of logical syntax. In the *Tractatus*, Wittgenstein had sought to provide the most general conceptions possible with his commitment to the general form of propositions typifying this. Wittgenstein's conception of philosophical methodology changed substantially in the *Investigations*. He stressed that philosophy makes itself redundant by exposing the abuses of language which have generated it. Wittgenstein exclusively used grammatical investigation when considering philosophical problems as he regarded it as the only possible method which could clear up philosophical confusion. Philosophical inquiries do not require an explanation, but they need a sense. Wittgenstein thought that there is not a philosophical method but methods just as there are different therapies. A fundamental tenet of his philosophical methodology was that once a mistake had been identified it should be returned to repeatedly from a variety of different perspectives so that evermore mistaken assumptions were exposed. In opposition to the *Tractatus* he claimed that the craving for generality was a primary cause of philosophical problems and that it must be resisted.

Wittgenstein's conception of how language functions altered dramatically from the *Tractatus* onwards. The introduction of new ideas, such as language games and family resemblance, clearly reflected Wittgenstein's transformed perspective about language. Language changed from being an *a priori* deduction in the *Tractatus* about the nature of any possible sign system to looking and seeing how words are used. He firmly rejected the idea that there are *a priori* ways of dealing with and understanding language. From the middle period onwards, the concept of grammar was used and it differs from the notion of logical syntax in many important respects. One aspect of his rejection of the metaphysics of the *Tractatus* was his espousal of the arbitrariness of grammar. A significant alteration in Wittgenstein's conception of language was his view that the rules of grammar do not reflect the truths of metaphysics. His differing view of the relationship of language to metaphysics in the *Tractatus* and his later work is central for understanding his idea that grammar is arbitrary. The sense in which grammar is arbitrary is that the linguistic community's grammatical rules cannot be correct or accord truthfully with the facts. What the linguistic community says accords with the facts if it is true but the truths are not themselves grammatical rules. The Augustinian picture is based on the idea that words are the names of objects and the meaning of each one is the object which it stands for. Sentences are combinations of names. Understanding the meaning of a sentence is knowing what is described by it. This knowledge arises from comprehending what the words stand for and how they are combined. In the *Tractatus* elementary propositions consisted of names and the meaning of a name was identified with the object it represented. Wittgenstein later argued that the *Tractatus* was underpinned by the Augustinian picture of language and criticized these views through an attack on this picture. He argued that the meaning of a name is not an object of any kind and the conception of meaning as use replaced the picture theory of meaning. Wittgenstein stressed the connection between the use and meaning of language. He was not offering a general theory that the meaning of a word is its use but was rather drawing attention to an important feature of our linguistic practice. He employed his ideas about meaning to focus attention upon the community's ordinary linguistic practices and thereby to assist in the dissolution of the puzzling theoretical questions about the notion of meaning.

The distinction between the notions of nonsense and senseless was confined to the *Tractatus* and disappeared in the later work. The rules of logical syntax were related to this distinction between the notions of nonsense and senseless. Nonsensical propositions violated the rules of logical syntax. Senseless propositions do not say anything. The rules of logical syntax demarcated the bounds of sense by unequivocally fixing whether and what sense any possible combination of signs made. Nonsense was unequivocal and circumstance independent. In the later work the distinction between sense and nonsense characteristically depended upon circumstances. Wittgenstein thought that there was not a single invariant concept of sense or nonsense which is governed by the rules of syntax and semantics and is entirely circumstance independent. The corollary to this is that what counts as nonsense can be variously characterized depending upon the circumstances of the sentence. It follows that there are as many different ideas of nonsense as there are reasons in different circumstances for asserting that some expression is nonsensical.

The *Tractatus* claimed that all symbol systems including natural languages must conform to the rules of logical syntax. On this conception language has a common essence. Later Wittgenstein came to think that an analogy with family resemblance could be used to explain the connection between particular employments of the same word. In a case of family resemblance the phenomena in question had no properties in common which ensured that the same word was applied to all of them. Wittgenstein did not just apply the concept of family resemblance to words in language as he thought that language itself was a case of it. It cannot be stated what is common to all language and indeed to seek the essence of language would be misguided. One of the fundamental principles of the *Tractatus* was that language was a kind of hidden calculus. Wittgenstein thought that the rules of logical syntax govern natural language even though speakers are unaware of them. The grammar of a natural language hid the complex system of rules which underpinned it and these rules could be exposed by logical analysis. The grammatical forms of sentences may disguise the actual logical form of the proposition expressed but the rules of logical syntax would display this logical form. In his later writings, Wittgenstein's emphasis upon the ordinary aspects of meaning sought to weaken the philosophical fascination of this model of language. A significant distinction for Wittgenstein was that between being in accord with and following a rule. To follow a rule an individual must intend to follow it and be able to invoke it in an account of his practice if required. He objected to the calculus model on the grounds that speakers were not acquainted with the strict rules of the calculus and therefore could not be following them. The fact that the linguistic behaviour of speakers could be correlated with the rules of the calculus does not reveal that the underlying structure of language is governed by such rules. Wittgenstein thought that the only legitimate philosophical role of the calculus model was as an object of comparison.

Wittgenstein accepted a commitment to the determinacy of sense in the *Tractatus* but in his later work he rejected it. He is sometimes mistakenly interpreted as regarding vagueness as desirable and an alternative to adhering to the determinacy of sense. The reason this interpretation is unsatisfactory is that Wittgenstein did not define vagueness as the absence of the determinacy of sense because he thought that there was no such thing. He criticized the presuppositions which lay behind the commitment to this determinacy of sense. One of these was the view in the *Tractatus* that bivalence and bipolarity were essential features of language. Wittgenstein also challenged the position arising from the book's approach to meaning that any particular instance of vagueness could not be contained and would affect any parts of language logically conjoined with it. Wittgenstein repudiated the *Tractatus'* idea that definition which provided the necessary and sufficient conditions for applying a word was the only adequate kind. In his later work he claimed that a complete definition of word would not result in a more precise understanding of every sentence in which the word occurred. Wittgenstein argued that many expressions are not explained by the specification of necessary and sufficient conditions for their application. He claimed that there was no such thing as an explanation of meaning of an expression which ruled out the very possibility of vagueness about its application in any conceivable circumstances. The difference between a precise and an imprecise explanation of meaning is not independent of context and purpose. This was related to Wittgenstein's contention that community consensus about acceptable practices of explanation is sufficient to distinguish correct from incorrect explanations. It was central to his conception of explanations of meaning that all forms of explanation of meaning are adequate. Wittgenstein stressed that diverse explanations of the same word can be equally acceptable. He thought that there was considerable diversity in the kinds of explanation of meaning, as these ranged from ostensive definition to explanation by paraphrase and explanation through examples.

The initial focus of Wittgenstein's later dissatisfaction with logical atomism was his rejection of his former view that elementary propositions were logically independent. He was no longer optimistic about finding the necessary analysis to solve the difficulty of the manifest incompatibility of apparently unanalysable statements which is a generalized version of the colour exclusion problem. As a result of this Wittgenstein adopted the position that not all cases of incompatibility can be reduced to instances of logical impossibility and in doing he diverged from the *Tractatus*. Subsequently he introduced the conception of propositional systems to deal with the difficulties created by his realization that elementary propositions could not be logically independent. However, he soon became unhappy with them on the grounds that the scope for their application was limited to values which were determinate instances of some range that could clearly be fixed. A further problem was that even in these particular cases the conception of propositional systems disregarded the fact that not all values which were determinate instances of some range that could clearly be fixed had the same combinatorial possibilities in common. In the *Tractatus* Wittgenstein had regarded the only necessity as logical necessity and the only impossibility as logical impossibility. In the later work he adopted a radically different approach to necessity. Wittgenstein's central idea was that what philosophers term necessary propositions are characteristically arbitrary grammatical rules. He was interested in the use of sentences when considering necessity and thought that the distinction between necessary and contingent propositions is related to their use. In the *Tractatus* Wittgenstein had criticized the logicist definition of numbers and submitted a constructive alternative according to which the natural numbers represented stages in the execution of a logical operation. In his later writings he applied the notions of grammar and rules that he had developed to claim that mathematical propositions were grammatical rules. He maintained that the meaning of a mathematical proposition is constituted by its proof but that it was misleading to think that a proof demonstrates that a mathematical proposition is true.

CHAPTER 4

THE MIDDLE PERIOD

CRITICISM OF THE *TRACTATUS*

The middle period represented a distinct stage in Wittgenstein's thought. After he returned to Cambridge in 1929 he sought to correct what he perceived as the errors of his earlier writings. Although this was one of the most productive periods of his life he was constantly dissatisfied with the results of his work. Between 1929 and 1933 Wittgenstein's views significantly changed with his ideas undergoing frequent and important modification. The published works and *Nachlass* material dating from this time indicate important progressions in the development of his ideas. Other significant records include notes on his lectures taken by Moore from 1930–33 (Moore, 1959a) and by Lee from 1930–32 (*L*). The result of the alterations in Wittgenstein's thought were primarily new conceptions of language and philosophical methodology. During this period many of the notions in the *Tractatus* were employed but the setting in which they were utilized radically modified their import.

The middle period is important for interpreting the later work, especially the *Investigations*, because it shows the development of major ideas found there. Compressed presentations and passages on notions and themes in these subsequent writings are evident in more expanded forms in the middle period, such as in the *Blue and Brown Books*. The growth in scholarship on the middle period has revealed how complex and difficult its interpretation is. The aim is to draw some of the broad contours of Wittgenstein's thought at this time so that the reader can profitably approach specialist works about this. A key issue is the extent to which ideas that are found in Wittgenstein's texts from the middle period onwards are ones which he reasonably firmly adhered to for any length of time. This frequent alteration of his positions means that it is important to locate other sources which can be used to correlate Wittgenstein's changing ideas. Probably the most significant one is the work of Friedrich Waismann. However, there is controversy over the value of Waismann's work as a source for interpreting Wittgenstein's views. The nature of the relationship between their work bears upon this matter. Waismann's book *Logik, Sprache, Philosophie* was the consummation of a prolonged collaborative spell with Wittgenstein.[1] During this period Waismann's main objective was to create a systematic exposition of the latter's philosophy by trying to connect together into an orderly entirety the material from typescripts and conversations with him. Under the circumstances in which Waismann worked with Wittgenstein it would not have been easy, to say the least, for the former to be appraised of the latter's shifting positions. Wittgenstein was worried about the potential corruption of his ideas in the book. An important example of the differences between them which fuelled Wittgenstein's concern was how the *Tractatus* should be viewed. Waismann took Wittgenstein's work at this time to be an expansion and variation of the basic concepts of the *Tractatus*. However, Wittgenstein regarded much of this later writing as conflicting with a substantial part of the positions propounded there. Gradually their collaboration broke down with Waismann ultimately writing *Logik, Sprache, Philosophie* alone. The trouble is that in Waismann's *Logik, Sprache, Philosophie* it is difficult to be certain whether he reported precisely what Wittgenstein thought. The progressions of Wittgenstein's ideas are mirrored in Waismann's records but the developments are not invariably at one.

The initial phase of Wittgenstein's repudiation of logical atomism emerged in his 1929 article 'Some Remarks on Logical Form'. However, he later disowned it with a clear indication of this being his 1933 letter to the journal *Mind*. At this time Wittgenstein was still working within the broad conception of logical analysis presented in the *Tractatus*. In 'Some Remarks on Logical Form' a growing sense of dissatisfaction with particular fundamental aspects of the book's account of logical atomism was evident. However, prior to his criticisms Wittgenstein stated some significant tenets of logical atomism. He remarked that there was a temptation to think that atomic propositions had the form of subject and predicate and relational propositions. This temptation was mistaken because the true character of elementary propositions was that they are immediate combinations of names. The forms of elementary propositions could not be deduced from the character of propositions in natural language and logical analysis was required to expose their nature. The limited number of forms in natural language corresponded to a multiplicity of different logical forms. The focus of Wittgenstein's dissatisfaction with logical atomism was his rejection of his former view that elementary propositions were logically independent. He was no longer optimistic about finding the necessary analysis to solve the difficulty of the manifest incompatibility of apparently unanalysable statements which is a generalized version of the colour exclusion problem. (For his later solution to the problem of colour exclusion see the discussion of necessity in Chapter 6.) As a result of this Wittgenstein adopted the position that not all cases of incompatibility can be reduced to instances of logical impossibility and in doing he diverged from the *Tractatus*. The reason for his abandonment of the idea that elementary propositions are logically independent appears to have arisen from investigation of incompatibilities involving the attribution of qualities that admit of gradation, such as the brightness of a shade of colour. For example, consider the sentences 'A has exactly one degree of brightness' and 'A has exactly two degrees of brightness'. The problem is to provide analyses of these sentences that expose the logical impossibility of their both being true together. What Wittgenstein took to be the most plausible solution adapted the system of propositions described in the *Tractatus* through the addition of numeric variables. Elementary propositions would have functions which take the form 'E has n degrees of property P' and they would return a true proposition for only one value of the variable n. At any time not more than one such proposition could be true and a consequence of this is that the tenet of the logical independence of elementary propositions had to fall. Wittgenstein now thought that something having both exactly one and exactly two degrees of brightness was an irreducibly mathematical impossibility.

Wittgenstein's second phase of dismantling logical atomism involved a far more radical break with the conception of logical analysis presupposed in the *Tractatus*. He regarded the fundamental intellectual error of the book as being that of dogmatism (*WWK*, pp. 182–4). In the *Tractatus* the task of logical analysis had been to uncover logical form hidden by natural language. Wittgenstein offered a perspective on his previous conception of logical analysis (*PG*, p. 211):

> Formerly, I myself spoke of a 'complete analysis', and I used to believe that philosophy had to give a definitive dissection of propositions so as to set out clearly all their connections and remove all possibilities of misunderstanding. I spoke as if there was a calculus in which such a dissection would be possible. I vaguely had in mind something like the definition that Russell had given for the definite article . . .

He now began to question this conception of logical analysis. One aspect of his criticism was directed against the idea that it was possible in principle to specify things that were not yet known provided logical analysis was carried far enough. Wittgenstein thought that philosophical methodology should not allow for gaps between questions and answers such that answers could be found later. He was clear that he had broken this methodological precept in the *Tractatus* despite his awareness that philosophy did not aim at developing theories and discovering new facts. Wittgenstein remarked that 'The answers to philosophical questions must never be surprising. In philosophy you cannot discover anything. I myself, however, had not clearly enough understood this [in the *Tractatus*] and offended against it' (*WWK*, p. 182). An example of this failure to observe the methodological principle against philosophical discovery was that further details about elementary propositions could be subsequently specified. Wittgenstein also regarded the view that it was possible in principle to discover objects provided logical analysis was carried far enough as breaking this precept. During the composition of the *Tractatus*, Wittgenstein thought that objects were 'that for which there is neither existence nor non-existence' (*PR*, p. 72) as they could be referred to without any possibility of their not existing. At that time, he had not decided upon what would be regarded as an instance of a simple object and set the question aside as one to be settled later once further progress in logical analysis had been made. Wittgenstein now viewed this attitude as erroneous (*AWL*, p. 11).

Wittgenstein had realized that elementary propositions could not be logically independent. Propositions were no longer regarded as pictures which were individually compared with reality but instead were matched against reality in groups. Wittgenstein used the metaphor of graduating marks on a ruler for this conception of regarding propositions as being in groups. He thought that, for example, establishing x is 2 centimetres long established that it is not 7 metres long and similarly, for instance, that a point in an individual's visual field being red implied that it was neither orange nor green and so on. From these kinds of analysis Wittgenstein developed the position that propositions formed proposition systems. These systems were sets of propositions such that propositions belonging to them excluded each other not upon truth-functional grounds but because of the concepts which occurred in them (*WWK*, pp. 63f. and *PR*, ch. VIII). The scope for propositions to mutually exclude each other in these systems was simultaneously a logical space of possibilities. For example, black could be grouped with red but 7 metres long could not (*PR*, pp. 75–7). A consequence of this was that logical syntax became even more complex than before. This provoked Russell's complaint that the conceptions in the *Philosophical Remarks* would make 'mathematics and logic almost incredibly difficult' (letter Russell to Moore, 5.5.30). Another problem with the adoption of proposition systems was that their logical analysis yielded several surprising results. For example, one of these was that all propositions included expressions that denoted real numbers. Wittgenstein became dissatisfied with the conception of propositional systems on the grounds that the scope for their application was limited to values which were determinate instances of some range that could clearly be fixed (such as being 7 metres long in the case of length). A further problem was that even in these particular cases the conception of propositional systems disregarded the fact that not all values which were determinate instances of some range that could clearly be fixed had the same combinatorial possibilities in common.

What led Wittgenstein to abandon the analysis of generality in the *Tractatus* was his realization that he had failed adequately to think through the infinite case. He had proceeded as though the finite case could be used as a way of thinking about the infinite case, the details of which could be sorted out at a later date. Wittgenstein came to see his earlier attitude as resting on the mistake of confusing 'dots of laziness' with 'dots of infinitude'. The dots in a proposition such as 'sky is blue, water is blue . . .' were ones of laziness if they could be filled in given sufficient time and space and of infinitude if they marked an infinite gap which could not be filled. Wittgenstein was dissatisfied by the *Tractatus'* account of universal quantification as a conjunction except when the conjunction was clearly finite. For instance, statements about all numbers could clearly not be treated as conjunction of statements about each of the numbers (*WWK*, p. 45). The *Tractatus* implied that universal and existential quantification could be applied to any proposition. However, once it was evident that elementary propositions might not be logically independent, the possibility of one sort of logical operation no longer guaranteed the possibility of another sort. What makes sense in some instances does not necessarily make sense in all. Wittgenstein thought that the problem with the treatment of universal and existential quantification in the *Tractatus* was the mistaken supposition that every quantified proposition was analysable into a kind of logical conjunction or disjunction. He claimed that every system of propositions had its own rules for generality when he remarked that 'There are as many different "alls"' as there are sorts of propositions (*PG*, p. 269).

PHILOSOPHICAL REMARKS AND PHILOSOPHICAL GRAMMAR

Wittgenstein needed to secure funding to be able to continue his philosophical work. The work which was published as the *Philosophical Remarks* was quickly compiled from a number of typescripts in order to support his application for a five-year fellowship at Trinity College, Cambridge. However, Wittgenstein's major efforts were devoted to the composition of an intended book based upon some of his manuscripts of the time. The 'Big Typescript' of 1933 was the nearest he came to completing a draft for it. It comprised 768 pages in conjunction with an annotated table of contents. This work contained his later conceptions about meaning, intentionality and the nature of philosophy. About one third of it focused upon the philosophy of mathematics and in doing so it dealt with many of same topics as the later *Remarks on the Foundations of Mathematics*. The *Philosophical Grammar* was compiled from sections of the original 'Big Typescript' and Wittgenstein's first two revisions of it.

Wittgenstein's treatment of epistemology prior to *On Certainty* primarily occurred in the middle period and was concerned with verificationist concepts. However, this interest only had a small role in his work at that time and this indicates that he had very little interest in what is regarded as traditional epistemology. Much of the prominent treatment of verificationist notions is found in *Ludwig Wittgenstein und der Wiener Kreis* and *Logik, Sprache, Philosophie* which reflected his involvement with the Vienna Circle at the time. He made an early application of the verification principle to both empirical statements and mathematical propositions but later he rejected this view. Wittgenstein's attitude to verificationism is relevant as a number of philosophers have argued that his emphasis on language and human behaviour is best understood as a form of anti-realism. Anti-realism focuses upon assertion conditions rather than truth conditions for the use of language. One objection to an anti-realist interpretation is that Wittgenstein was interested in understanding what makes sense and would have regarded both anti-realism and realism as species of misguided metaphysics. It is evident from his treatment of propositions and hypotheses that his verificationism is not a version of anti-realism.

During Wittgenstein's brief concern with verificationist notions, he differentiated between propositions which are genuinely propositions and hypothesis relations (*PR*, ch. XXII). The hypothesis relation was concerned with how propositions were connected to reality. His specific devotion of chapters in the *Philosophical Remarks* (XXII) and *Philosophical Grammar* (Part I, appendix, chapter 6) to the hypothesis relation suggests the import which the idea had in his thought at that time. A general problem when assessing Wittgenstein's perspective on the hypothesis relation is that his handling of it was not particularly lucidly expressed. An overall difficulty is that there is a lack of unity between the treatments of this relation in the *Philosophical Remarks* and *Philosophical Grammar*. This raises the question of which of these works is a more faithful representation of his ideas about the hypothesis relation.

The hypothesis relation was not a genuine proposition in the sense that a proposition was capable of being true or false. Wittgenstein remarked that if a hypothesis relation could not be definitely verified then it was not possible to verify it all and it had neither truth nor falsehood (*PR*, §226). This relation was not susceptible to decisive verification or directly measured against reality to settle its truth. Hypothesis relations were made more or less probable by evidence (*PR*, §225). However, it was not the case that aggregation of evidential backing would ensure that a hypothesis relation was certain. Evidence was linked to a hypothesis relation in a manner akin to the way in which points on a curve were connected to a curve. This linkage was a grammatical one and was not empirical in nature, as particular evidence making a hypothesis relation probable fixed in part the meaning of that relation (*PR*, §227). The hypothesis relation was used in several diverse contexts. Wittgenstein (*WWK*) employed this relation to connect observation statements to scientific theories. He held that an observation statement at most was evidence for the hypothesis relation which it sustains and the relation is the firmest tie coupling observations to theories. A different application of the hypothesis relation was to relate statements about the material world to those about sense data. The reports of sense data were clearly used to support hypothesis relations concerning statements in regard to the material world (*PR*, §230). The concept of a hypothesis relation also found a role in Wittgenstein's philosophy of mind and as part of his consideration of the problem of other minds. The usage of this relation was to couple behavioural descriptions to other minds. Hypothesis relations with respect to statements about other minds were upheld by behavioural descriptions (*PR*, §64). In Wittgenstein's work in 1932–3 there was a gradual reduction in the extent of the application of the hypothesis relation which eventually resulted in its disappearance by the time he wrote the *Blue and Brown Books*. In that work, he generally rejected the notion of the hypothesis relation as an incoherent one (*BB*, p. 48).

The hypothesis relation had connections to Wittgenstein's brief commitment to methodological solipsism. His version of methodological solipsism was the position that basic propositions were ones about experience and claims about the mental states of other people were logical constructions produced from observations of their behaviour. The reason that this position was a kind of methodological solipsism was that the only experiences which were recognized were one's own. He thought that the only experientially derived propositions that could be rendered in terms of instant and decisive verification were abstractions from first person present tense psychological statements in which the first person no longer had a role (*WWK*, pp. 49f. and *PR*, pp. 88–90). Given this, claims about other people's experiences must be produced out of statements about their behaviour. However, by 1932–3 Wittgenstein held that it was mistaken to regard statements about other minds as hypotheses which were incapable of conclusive verification and that other people's experiences were logical constructions derived from evidence of behaviour.

Wittgenstein accepted Frege's commitment to the determinacy of sense in the *Tractatus* but in his later work he rejected it. He is sometimes mistakenly interpreted as regarding vagueness as desirable and an alternative to adhering to the determinacy of sense. The reason this interpretation is unsatisfactory is that Wittgenstein did not define vagueness as the absence of the determinacy of sense because he thought that there was no such thing. Much of his writing about vagueness and determinacy of sense was aimed at undermining the distorting effects of the assumption that sense had to be determinate. For example, this assumption distorted the ordinary notion of what it was to be vague. Wittgenstein held that terms such as 'exact' were ones of approval and their opposites ones of disapproval provided they were understood in terms of the usual concept of vagueness. He criticized the presuppositions which lay behind the commitment to this determinacy of sense. One of these was the view that bivalence and bipolarity were essential features of language. Wittgenstein also challenged the position arising from the *Tractatus'* approach to meaning that any particular instance of vagueness could not be contained and would affect any parts of language logically conjoined with it.

Wittgenstein argued that if the commitment to the determinacy of sense was construed as the elimination of not just vagueness but the very possibility of it when applying expressions then such a demand could not be met. He claimed that there is an indeterminate list of the circumstances which cover the rules for the use of words. It cannot be proved that circumstances are normal (*PI*, §183 and *Z*, §118). Wittgenstein thought that abnormal circumstances can be recognized and explained (*Z*, §118). He asserted that in normal circumstances the rules for the use of a word are clear whilst in abnormal circumstances nothing rules a usage in or out absolutely (*PI*, §142). For example, it is not so difficult to think of circumstances in which normal rules are not appropriate. An instance of this is Wittgenstein's treatment of the notion of personal identity (*BB*, pp. 61f.) where he examined the idea of everyone having bodies which were identical. Another case is that of a variant of the game of chess where only the pawns can be moved and when there are no pawns or legal moves with them left the game is decided by rolling a dice to see which player has the highest throw. It is clear that the normal rules of chess are inappropriate here.

Wittgenstein repudiated Frege and the *Tractatus'* attitudes towards the partial definition of words. Frege's principle of completeness of definition required of the explanation of a concept word that it solely fixes for every object whether or not each object comes under the concept (1962, §56). In contrast to this Wittgenstein claimed that a complete definition of a word would not result in a more precise understanding of every sentence in which the word occurred. One way in which Frege formulated his principle of the completeness of definition was as a metaphorical characterization of a concept as a sharp boundary drawn on an infinite plane which was compared to an area. Wittgenstein clearly criticized this view when he repudiated the claim that an area with vague boundaries cannot be regarded as an area at all (*PG*, §32, *PI*, §§68f., 71 and 76). He held that vagueness is sometimes useful (*PI*, §71) as all that was required is definition for some instances. Against this position it might be objected that there could be borderline cases of vagueness but a precise determination of what comprises such instances is required. In response to this Wittgenstein argued that this attempt at precise determination leads to a regress as the border can never be fixed exactly (*PI*, §88 and *Z*, §§441f.). He argued that there was no such thing as an explanation of meaning of an expression which ruled out the very possibility of vagueness about its application in any conceivable circumstances (*PI*, §87). Wittgenstein remarked that as no single ideal of precision has been stipulated it is not known 'what we should be supposed to imagine under this head – unless you yourself lay down what is to be so called. But you will find it difficult to hit upon such a convention; at least any that satisfies you' (*PI*, §88). One of the points here is that the difference between a precise and an imprecise explanation of meaning is not independent of context and purpose (*PI*, §§88 and l00). An imprecise explanation is one which cannot be understood in a particular context.

One of the fundamental principles of the *Tractatus* was that language was a kind of calculus. Between 1929 and 1933 Wittgenstein compared speaking a language to operating a logical or mathematical calculus (*PR*, ch. XX and *PG*, p. 57) and made use of this analogy. However, he differed from the *Tractatus* in thinking that the rules of the calculus were arbitrary, which is to say that they could not be correct or accord truthfully with the facts. Wittgenstein claimed that it was the method of application which differentiated language from a calculus that was not applied (*WWK*, pp. 103–5 and 124). As the importance of the requirement about the application of the signs in a calculus became evident he criticized the calculus model of language. This was one of the reasons that pre-cipitated his 1931 replacement of the notion of logical syntax with that of grammar. A number of considerations led Wittgenstein to repudiate considering language from the point of view of examining a calculus. His remarks can be interpreted as citing the calculus model as a perspective on language which gave rise to questions about the legitimacy of normal linguistic practices. Wittgenstein remarked that the comparison of language with a calculus was mis-leading and rejected its commitment to regarding language as a system of precise and rigid rules. He thought that its perspective was a 'one-sided way of looking at language' (*BB*, p. 25 and *PG*, p. 68) and that language was not used or taught according to strict rules. Furthermore, the calculus model did not match the actual practices of explaining meaning. Wittgenstein's emphasis upon the ordinary aspects of meaning sought to weaken the philosophical fascination of this model of language. He also objected to the calculus model on the grounds that speakers were not acquainted with the strict rules of the calculus and therefore could not be following them. The fact that the linguistic behaviour of speakers could be correlated with the rules of the calculus does not reveal that the underlying structure of language is governed by such rules. Wittgenstein thought that the only legitimate philosophical role of the calculus model was as an object of comparison.

BLUE AND BROWN BOOKS

Wittgenstein's views had substantially changed by the time the 'Big Typescript' was composed. As soon as it was finished he became dissatisfied with it and significantly revised it. The final revision of the 'Big Typescript' was virtually contemporary with the *Blue Book* and had very strong affinities with it in a number of ways. More than 200 remarks in the *Investigations* were present in the 'Big Typescript' or the later revisions. The *Blue Book* was notes which Wittgenstein dictated to five of his students in Cambridge in 1933–4 and in 1934–5 he dictated the *Brown Book*. From 1934–6 Wittgenstein devoted considerable attention to private experience and sense data in preparation for his lectures on this in 1936. This was an important stage in his philosophical development and indicated the start of his concern with the philosophy of mind which subsequently became a major theme in his work. This interest in the philosophy of mind later found a developed expression in the differences between first and third person present tense psychological statements and in the private language argument. Wittgenstein was unhappy with both the *Blue and Brown Books*. He thought for some time that he might publish the *Brown Book*. In 1936 he attempted a German revision and expansion of this (which was published as *Eine Philosophische Betrachtung*) that he subsequently abandoned as worthless. After this in 1936–7 Wittgenstein wrote the first part of what was the first version of what eventually became the *Philosophical Investigations*. The typescript produced from this covered approximately the first 189 sections of the *Investigations* but differed in many respects.

When approaching Wittgenstein's later work the *Blue and Brown Books* are often recommended as a good place to start and it is also frequently suggested that the *Investigations* should be read in conjunction with them. One of the reasons for this is that the *Blue and Brown Books* are the most accessible of Wittgenstein's writings. This is because they were not as stylistically polished as the *Investigations* and so more context around plus argument in favour of his claims was supplied. The *Blue Book* seems to have the highest degree of continuity of all Wittgenstein's works. It is clear that discussions follow on from one another and thus where a topic was placed matters. The *Blue and Brown Books* fit more closely with the *Philosophical Remarks* and *Philosophical Grammar* than the *Investigations*. For example, regarding language as a calculus was an important theme in the first three works whilst it was not in the latter. Another case is that in the *Blue Book* Wittgenstein persistently discussed the idea of thinking as operating with signs (pp. 6, 12, and so on) but this notion was not treated at all in the *Investigations*. It is widely agreed that the *Blue and Brown Books* are different from Wittgenstein's later writings but the precise distinction and relationships between these works is controversial. A misleading oversimplification is to regard the *Blue and Brown Books* as simply preliminary studies for the *Investigations*[2] and they diverge from the latter in substantial ways. The complexity of the relationship between the *Blue and Brown Books* and the *Investigations* is readily evident in specialist literature about Wittgenstein's later work.

A key concept in Wittgenstein's later work and one that has gained wider philosophical currency is the notion of language game. From the middle period onwards he compared language with games and the point of the analogy was to draw attention to various similarities between language and games. A major objective was to demonstrate that language was a rule-governed activity. Unlike in the calculus model, this invocation of rules did not regard language as a system of precise and rigid rules but aimed at illustrating a different conception of the relationship between rules and language. Wittgenstein thought that language like games had rules which constituted it. The rules governing the operation of a word determined its meaning. The meaning of a word was learnt through its use in the same way that chess was learnt through understanding how the pieces can move. A proposition was conceived as a move in a language game and drew its significance from the game of which it was a part. The sense of such a proposition was its role in language (*PG*, p. 130 and *BB*, p. 42). These rules defined what made sense in the language and the game and in doing so defined it (*PG*, pp. 63 and 77). Another point of the game analogy was that language and games did not need to have an objective which was external to them. For example, the game of chess does not have a goal which lies outside the playing of the game. In that sense language and games could be autonomous activities (*PG*, p. 184 and *Z*, §320).

Wittgenstein extended the analogy between language and games to encompass language as a whole from 1932 onwards and the term 'language game' stemmed from this. He had been developing ideas about the flexibility and variety of language, the role of the linguistic community, and other new perspectives on language. The concept of language games was designed to capture and express these sorts of conceptions. Wittgenstein did not provide a general account of what a language game was as it was intended to encapsulate the fluidity, diversity and community orientated characteristics of language. He made a few remarks about language games but the notion was primarily elucidated through a host of examples. These examples did exhibit properties of language games even if the properties in question are not always immediately apparent. In the *Blue Book* the concept of language game was introduced as that of 'primitive forms of language' (p. 17) but the notion was not used in it. Wittgenstein did not treat language games in the same fashion in all his writings. Due to this there could not be a single conception of a language game in Wittgenstein. There were differences between how language games, when regarded in the sense of being a model for understanding language, are viewed in Wittgenstein's middle- and late-period work. An important consequence of these differences is that if his changing perspective on language games is to be taken seriously then language games cannot be properly treated by just one account. The *Brown Book* contained the most systematic treatment of language games. However, difficulties in interpreting it arise from the fact that on many occasions no clear philosophical context and motivation for the discussion of particular groups of language games was provided. However, it is possible to work out what these philosophical contexts were by examining themes about language which were of interest to Wittgenstein. In the book a large number of language games were invented and applied to classical metaphysical problems such as necessity and possibility, the nature of time as well as to the concepts of rule-following and language itself. It has been argued by many commentators that here the method of discussing invented language games was used excessively. In the *Brown Book*, there were analogues to distinct language games. For example, when Wittgenstein was inquiring into the connections of language games, he was interested in how actually existing and potential but non-existing language games might interact, such as in the treatment of whether someone can swim the river (*BB*, §49). In the *Brown Book*, Wittgenstein experimented with the ideas of seeing language games as miniature models of what language is, and the extent to which the language game method could provide an account of what language is. He created and analysed primitive language games in order to see if they yielded insights into particular characteristics of language. That is to say, these language games were intended as function objects of comparison, as the *Investigations* indicated (§§2–27), which would illuminate the more complex practices of ordinary language by bringing their features into sharp relief. Wittgenstein was not concerned with the notion of the completeness of language games in the *Brown Book*. In his later work, he tended to think that focusing on the completeness of language games obscured the way in which they should be used in the understanding of language because the goal of the philosopher is not completeness or exactness but the resolution of philosophical problems. In the *Investigations* Wittgenstein remarked that the term 'language game' was meant to emphasize the fact that speaking a language constituted part of an activity or a form of life (§23). He thought that the form of life comprised some of the wider context in which language occurred (see Chapter 6). In the same section of the *Investigations*, Wittgenstein stressed the sheer diversity of ordinary language games as these included reporting or speculating about an event, forming and testing a hypothesis, making up a story, reading it, guessing riddles, making a joke, translating, asking and thanking. Language games were also one of Wittgenstein's methods of philosophical therapy. In the *Investigations*, he thought that (invented) language games could illuminate our language by exhibiting similarities and differences with it. For example, a cause of philosophical problems is employing the words of one language game according to the rules of another. Invented language games could help to dispel this confusion because they showed the kinds of linguistic usage which gave rise to such difficulties.

The concept of family resemblance is a criticism of an aspect of the *Tractatus'* idea that definition which provided the necessary and sufficient conditions for applying a word was the only adequate kind. Wittgenstein came to think that an analogy with family resemblance could be used to explain the connection between particular employments of the same word. In a case of family resemblance[3] the phenomena in question had no properties in common which ensured that the same word was applied to all of them (*PG*, §35, *RPPI*, §923 and *PI*, §65). Wittgenstein remarked that (*PG*, §35):

> 'Understanding' is not the name of a single process accompanying reading or hearing, but of more or less interrelated processes against a background, or in a context, of facts of a particular kind, viz. the actual use of a learnt language or languages.
>
> The relationship between the members of a concept may be set up by the sharing of features which show up in the family of the concept, crossing and overlapping in very complicated ways.

There is a complicated overlapping and criss-crossing network of similarities (*PI*, §66). For instance, consider various cases of expectation (*BB*, p. 20) and the experience of being guided (*PI*, §§172–9). Wittgenstein realized that treating similarity as an absolute notion was incoherent and he emphasized that there was only similarity in a respect (*PI*, §67). A family resemblance word had distinct applications and the citing of relevant similarities justified the employment of the same word for all these different things. What provides a family resemblance word with its unity was the overlapping network of similarities (*PI*, §§67f.). Family resemblance concepts were not sharply bounded (*PI*, §§68f.). It seems that Wittgenstein's choice of the idea of game to show the notion of family resemblance was related to the analogy he postulated between language and games. The explanation of a family resemblance word was through paradigmatic examples (*PI*, §71), such as explaining the word 'game' by giving the instances of chess and football. There are similarities between games and thus it is possible to proceed by analogy when deciding whether to count something as a game or not (*PG*, §73). Generally speaking, Wittgenstein discussed certain concepts in terms of family resemblance in the middle period. The majority of these concepts were ones in the philosophy of mind. For instance, there were the treatments of the notions of understanding (*PG*, §35), ability (*BB*, pp. 115–17), and reading (*BB*, pp. 119–25). Wittgenstein illustrated a small part of the variety of the notion of ability when he considered the employment of expressions such as 'can' and 'to be able to'. He suggested that such usage had characteristic features which appeared in different combinations depending upon the circumstances (*BB*, p. 117). In the case of reading, he suggested that the explanation of the word was fundamentally comprised by the description of a selected set of examples which exhibited the characteristic feature of reading (*BB*, p. 125). Some similar themes can be perceived in his extended discussion of the concept of reading in the *Investigations*. Wittgenstein did not just apply the concept of family resemblance to words in language as he thought that language itself was a case of it. It cannot be stated what is common to all language and indeed to seek the essence of language would be misguided.

A concept which is primarily associated with the *Blue Book* is that of criteria, although the notion appeared in a wide variety of Wittgenstein's works. The meaning of the word 'criteria' and its philosophical significance remain the subject of controversy. There is almost no sustained discussion of it in Wittgenstein's writings with the notable exception of the famous passages towards the start of the *Blue Book*. He commented that (pp. 24f.):

Let us introduce two antithetical terms in order to avoid certain elementary confusions: To the question 'How do you know that so-and-so is the case?', we sometimes answer by giving '*criteria*' and sometimes by giving '*symptoms*'. If medical science calls angina an inflammation caused by a particular bacillus, and we ask in a particular case 'why do you say this man has got angina?'

then the answer 'I have found the bacillus so-and-so in his blood' gives us the criterion, or what we may call the defining criterion of angina. If on the other hand the answer was, 'His throat is inflamed', this might give us a symptom of angina. I call a 'symptom' a phenomenon of which experience has taught us that it coincided, in some way or other, with the phenomenon which is our defining criterion.

A difficulty raised by this passage is what the relationship between criteria and symptoms is supposed to be. Another problem is whether criteria are defining criteria and if not what is the term 'defining criterion' doing in this context? Wittgenstein proceeded to comment on the identification of criteria and symptoms (*BB*, p. 25):

In practice, if you were asked which phenomenon is the defining criterion and which is a symptom, you would in most cases be unable to answer this question except by making an arbitrary decision *ad hoc*. It may be practical to define a word by taking one phenomenon as the defining criterion, but we shall easily be persuaded to define the word by means of what, according to our first use, was a symptom. Doctors will use the names of diseases without ever deciding which phenomena are to be taken as criteria and which as symptoms; and this need not be a deplorable lack of clarity.

The identification of criteria and symptoms leads to the question of how the fluctuation between the two is to be understood and the consequences this has for how the definitions of words should be regarded. How these issues arising from the passages are to be resolved is fundamentally connected to the position taken on whether there is a theory of criteria or not and if so what form it takes. The single largest division in the debate on criteria in Wittgenstein revolves around whether there is a theory of criteria or not. The vast majority of philosophers see him as laying down the basis for a theory of criteria which he did not fully or consistently develop but their interpretations of this vary widely. The opposing view is that any attempt to provide a theory of criteria would be committing a philosophical error. It is claimed that, in itself, the term 'criterion' does not provide a key to anything because it does not have a general meaning and neither is it part of some concealed theory. The attitude taken towards the question of there being a theory of criteria partly depends upon whether Wittgenstein's professed philosophical methodology and actual practice are regarded as consistent. The most widely accepted interpretation of criteria which propounds a theory is the non-inductive evidence view. It holds that the concept of criteria links semantics and epistemology. The main tenets of the position are that a criterion holding between two propositions makes a contribution to the sense of both propositions, and the criteria relation is distinct from one of entailment. It is claimed that the criteria relation is based in grammar and thus if a proposition criterially supports another proposition, this support is independent of empirical evidence. This position maintains that if a proposition criterially supports another proposition and it is known that the former proposition is true, then it is fully justified to claim to know that latter proposition is true. Certainty is established by criterial support which is conclusive. Despite being the dominant theory, significant reservations have been voiced about whether this notion of a criterion is basically incoherent and if it is the best construal of the passages about criteria in Wittgenstein's work. Issues about criteria have import beyond the notion itself as the concept of criteria is regarded as having a significant place in the philosophy of mind. For example, what secures knowledge of others' mental states is the connection between the sense of statements which ascribe states to individuals and what is taken to be evidence that an individual is in a particular state. If mental states do have criteria, which can be perceived then it is certain that when the criteria for a specific state obtain the state is present and that when they do not, the state is absent.

Wittgenstein considered issues about solipsism in the middle period and in his later work. Solipsism is the most extreme form of idealism which is the view that there is no material existence but there is non-material existence or as it is usually expressed, there are ideas. Solipsism is the position that the only thing which exists is the speaker and his states. When it is developed as far as possible, solipsism contends that the immediate current states of the speaker are the sole entity which exists. It is not possible for anything apart from the individual speaking and his states to exist. Assertions about the existence of anything other than the speaker and his states, if they are to be intelligible, must be handled as being a convenient mode of expression and nothing more. Given this outlook everything apart from the speaker and his states is just part of the external world and has an equal claim to existence. For example, minds and material objects have an equal claim. Wittgenstein's general approach to handling solipsism was to claim that solipsism was mistaking grammatical rules for metaphysical assertions. For example, in the solipsist, idealist, and realist debate the proponents may dispute the case of having pain (*BB*, pp. 58f. and *PI*, §§402f.). The solipsist claims that he has the only real pain. One position is taken to contradict the legitimacy of the other because the proponents think that they are dealing with conflicting metaphysical truths. The proponents of these divergent views are giving rules of grammar whilst contending that a metaphysical truth is being provided. In each case different grammatical rules for having pain are being employed. Wittgenstein's overall attack upon solipsism took the form of identifying the particular components which make up the solipsist position. For instance, some parts of the solipsist account are that the speaker is privileged and the present moment is unique. He aimed to show the problems which each component has and to demonstrate that the meaningful usage of each component assumes that a collection of circumstances which solipsism disallows hold. A case of this is that the solipsist's conceptual innovation about what counts as real pain is being presented as or appears to be a new discovery, but what is actually happening is that new grammatical rules are being introduced or called for. The solipsist who contends that he has the only real pain no longer wishes to use the ordinary grammatical rules which apply to pain. For instance, the employment of any rules of grammar which permit the ascription of genuine pain to others is rejected. The first point to note is that the solipsist has invoked ordinary grammatical rules to support his position and simultaneously denied the intelligibility of certain grammatical contrasts which are essential to the application of these rules. The point is that an expression such as 'my pain' can only make a meaningful claim in a language where it can be contrasted with 'his pain' (or something similar). It is not a significant expression in a language where 'my pain' is equated with 'there is pain' (*PR*, p. 85 and *BB*, pp. 71f.) (as according to the solipsist it is only I who can have genuine pain). In effect the solipsist has undertaken what might be thought of as grammatical sleight of hand as the sense of his claim that he has the only real pain presupposes the grammatical rules which he professes to reject. It follows that the solipsist's position is incoherent. Similar kinds of strategies were evident in Wittgenstein's discussion of the idea that the present moment is unique. In this case solipsism takes the form of maintaining that whenever anything is perceived it is always I who perceive it and it is my present experience that is perceived and furthermore that as the sole reality is my present experience I am 'the vessel of life' (*BB*, p. 65). Wittgenstein argued that although the solipsist claims to have discovered the metaphysical truth that the world is indeed identical with his experiences once again all that has really happened is that a new form of grammatical rule has been recommended.

CHAPTER 5

AIMS AND METHODS OF PHILOSOPHICAL THERAPY

OBJECTIVES

Wittgenstein's view of the nature of philosophical inquiry played a central role in his later work. The particular character of philosophy does not lie in the topics it covers but in the nature of philosophical questions and their solutions. For Wittgenstein philosophical inquiry is not a profound investigation into the foundations of reality or the most general of the sciences. One way in which he distinguished science from philosophy, is that the former seeks to discover novel facts about the nature of reality whilst the latter does not aim at any sort of discovery at all (*PI*, §109). Philosophical propositions are not factual in nature regardless of the extent to which they seem to resemble statements of scientific fact. Their particular character and differences with other kinds of propositions should be made evident. Philosophy makes itself redundant by exposing the abuses of language which have generated it (*PI*, §§109 and 255). 'The real discovery is the one that makes me capable of stopping doing philosophy when I want to' (*PI*, §133) and is that of achieving the clarity which dissolves philosophical problems. This dissolution is achieved by the removal of the confusions which create the problems of philosophy. Wittgenstein remarked that his aim was to 'shew the fly the way out of the fly-bottle' (*PI*, §309). He thought that progress in philosophy required painstaking analysis with constant attention to the details of the inquiry. It is necessary to find errors and to demonstrate how they have arisen. The idea that the role of philosophy is to eliminate confusion is significant. It applies to any kind of philosophical thinking including that encountered in the course of scientific and other kinds of enquiry. For many philosophers the idea that the function of philosophy is removing confusion is disappointing because it appears to decrease the challenge and interest of the subject. Wittgenstein commented that the difficulty of philosophy is not reduced by his approach because it must be as complicated as the knots in our thinking which it unties (Z, §452 and PR, §2). Emerging from confusion can be a protracted and complex process (Z, §382). Philosophical problems are deep because they are rooted in the ways that human beings think and the same difficulties in different forms will recur endlessly. The routes into philosophical confusion are not finitely defined. The language in which philosophical problems are located alters and in doing so produces new sources of perplexity (which are underpinned by these deep-seated temptations to error). For example, the discovery of quantum mechanics and relativity theory in physics has created new questions in the philosophy of science. Philosophical progress is possible although it may be piecemeal (BB, p. 44). However, the fact that the recurrence of difficulties cannot be prevented means that the task of philosophy will never be completed (Z, §447). Wittgenstein's characterization of the objectives of philosophy in terms of eliminating confusion leads to the question of what positive value he attributed to the activity. Ryle addressed this matter when he famously asked what a fly that never got into a fly-bottle would miss. Wittgenstein thought that the practice of dissolving philosophical problems helped one to acquire the skill to resolve other similar kinds of difficulties and the conceptual clarity that is an objective in itself (PI, p. 206 and PR, Foreword).

The view that philosophical problems are based on conceptual confusions arising from misconstruing the meaning of words fundamentally shaped Wittgenstein's methodological commitments. He exclusively used grammatical investigation when considering philosophical problems as he regarded it as the only possible method which could clear up philosophical confusion. Philosophical inquiries do not require an explanation, but they need a sense. They deal with the limits of sense and the latter is fixed by rules for the employment of words. Wittgenstein claimed that philosophical problems often arose from breaking the rules of grammar. The resolution of philosophical problems is the origin of philosophy's involvement with grammatical rules. The philosopher's concern with grammatical rules is focused by philosophical questions. The point is that particular grammatical rules are not intrinsically more interesting or significant than others: what is worthy of attention depends upon the problem in question and if this changes so may the rules which are being examined. The elucidation and organization of grammatical rules can dissolve philosophical problems. Distinctive features of philosophy's attitude to grammar can be highlighted if this is compared to the linguist's interest in grammar. Wittgenstein was not claiming that there is a special sort of grammar which philosophers concern themselves with and then there is ordinary grammar but rather that there are two sorts of focus upon grammatical rules which are shaped by divergent goals. The philosopher and the linguist handle grammatical issues differently because of their differing objectives. The linguist strives to produce a precise and extensive grammar for a language(s). For example, he may classify all the irregular verbs. Wittgenstein stressed that the philosopher is not concerned with either of the linguist's aims. A rigorous or comprehensive treatment of grammar is possible but this is frequently not relevant to the business of philosophy (Z, §464). This is because philosophy attends to grammar in order to dissolve philosophical problems and does not aim to generate a grammar as such. This point shows why Wittgenstein did not regard the difference between syntax and semantics or the distinctions between various parts of language given by traditional descriptive grammar as important to the philosopher (although he may pay attention to these matters in the pursuit of philosophical clarity). He noted that different philosophical questions will produce varying grammatical clarifications which dissolve the problem. Given that each classification of grammar is specific to the philosophical problem under consideration there is no such thing as the whole of the grammar with which philosophy should be concerned. Wittgenstein thought that the philosopher is interested in circumscribing sense and in how the bounds of sense which are of relative concern to a philosophical inquiry have been contravened. He mostly resolved philosophical problems by pointing out how they have broken grammatical rules. The reason for Wittgenstein's approach echoed the *Tractatus'* distinction between saying and showing. It is not possible to describe the limits of sense because there is nothing which lies beyond the boundaries of sense to be characterized. If these limits could be articulated then the negation of their articulation would constitute sense but if it did then the articulation would not be characterizing the limits of sense. Wittgenstein thought that a statement that has contravened the bounds of sense, which are determined by the grammatical rules, is a piece of nonsense.

Wittgenstein commented that a 'philosophical problem has the form: "I don't know my way about"' (*PI*, §123). He emphasized that there are no new facts to be found out by philosophy and it is only possible to have new insights into old facts. Philosophers have all the facts they require in front of them and the decisive move is their rearrangement (*PI*, §109). Wittgenstein claimed that philosophy leaves everything as it is (*PI*, §124), that is, appropriate descriptions which resolve philosophical problems succeed by showing how they are created. For example, philosophers notice particular differences in the employment of ordinary words that seem to require a theoretical explanation about the phenomena the words refer to but what is needed is merely a description of the different uses of those words. Wittgenstein held that philosophers should not supply a theory nor provide explanations. He remarked that: 'Philosophy simply puts everything before us, and neither explains nor deduces anything. – Since everything lies open to view there is nothing to explain' (*PI*, §126). Explanation is only possible if the idea of getting behind the rules of grammar is intelligible since it would then be possible to provide a deeper ground for these rules. However, this cannot be done and the rules cannot be correct or accord truthfully with the facts because grammar is arbitrary (see Chapter 6). Any deeper explanation would just be a further grammatical rule which stands in the same relation to linguistic usage as the rules that it supposedly explains. It follows that philosophy must be flat in the sense that there are no explanatory or argumentative hierarchies. Wittgenstein commented that the 'work of the philosopher consists in assembling reminders for a particular purpose' (*PI*, §127). Collecting reminders about the actual use of words contributes to the resolution of philosophical problems. The central task of philosophy is both to make one aware of the temptation to advance general theses and to show how to overcome this. Wittgenstein argued that the nature of philosophy ensures that there are no theses or conclusions in philosophy (*PI*, §128). That which could properly be called the end of a philosophical proof does not exist. There are grammatical remarks that play the role of synoptic descriptions in which grammatical truisms are drawn together and related to a particular philosophical problem. For example, if the comment 'an "inner process" stands in need of outward criteria' (*PI*, §580) is taken as a synoptic description it is pulling together and interconnecting the linguistic community's grammatical truisms about inner processes and their behavioural expressions. However, these descriptions are not argumentative premises. Their usefulness is to be measured by how effective they are in dissolving problems and promoting philosophical understanding. If there were theses in philosophy they would be trivial, in the sense that no one would disagree with them (*PI*, §128). For example, the assertion that one is aware of noises because one hears them is not a claim which would be regarded as a philosophical achievement. Philosophical progress consists in removing the confusions which prevent recognition of these trivialities (and in obtaining a better understanding of non-philosophical propositions). There are a variety of methods for achieving the dissolution of philosophical problems (*PI*, §133) and these will be considered in the next section.

A controversial issue is how Waismann's own conception of philosophy, especially that presented in his article 'How I See Philosophy', should be regarded as a source for understanding Wittgenstein's philosophical methodology. He termed it 'our method' to the extent which Wittgenstein and others shared it. There is dispute over whether Waismann's conception should be attributed to Wittgenstein or be regarded as opposed to it. There are a number of major differences between the account of Wittgenstein's philosophical methodology presented above and an account of this methodology which is founded upon Waismann's conception.[1] The latter account claims that the objective of philosophy is not the attainment of clarity and the elimination of confusion but is instead that of acquiring insight and seeing new aspects. A philosophical argument cannot force assent but instead provides a new perspective for seeing things. (Indeed this methodology does not even aim to show how philosophy must be done and tolerates other differing perspectives on the character of philosophical inquiry.) There is a very strong emphasis upon the idea that methodologically philosophy is akin to psychoanalysis.

Waismann's concern with regarding Wittgenstein's philosophical method in terms of an analogy with psychoanalysis resulted in interpretation according prominence to notions which are ignored in the majority of the standard interpretations of the latter's methodology. According to Waismann's conception discussions relative to an individual aim at dispelling the difficulties emanating from a philosopher's framework and habits of thought. Wittgenstein aimed to gain acknowledgement from those troubled by philosophical problems of what unconsciously influences them. The objective of therapy is wider than just particular mistakes and encompasses entire ways of thinking. The philosopher's admission of his puzzlement is indispensable for a correct diagnosis of the problems and his awareness of how his confusion has arisen is essential for the resolution of his difficulties. Wittgenstein developed this idea by claiming that philosophical concern with grammatical rules is always relative to a specific discussion with a philosopher of a particular problem. Therapy involves showing a philosopher the consequences of a commitment elicited from a philosophical confusion. For example, this confusion may be exposed by performing a comparison which demonstrates the inconsistency between what a philosopher claims to do when asked to describe his practice and what he actually does. There is no fact of the matter as to what these grammatical rules are. Wittgenstein claimed that rules should not be imposed on others. It is not possible to say anything in general about the detailed content of a particular grammatical investigation as each inquiry is shaped by the problem it is directed at. For example, the grammatical rules for arithmetic which are of philosophical interest are a philosopher's reasons for judging whether or not certain arithmetical calculations are correct. There is no such thing as delineating the grammatical rules for arithmetic which a philosopher attends to because of the relativity of interest of the grammatical rules to the philosophical problem and individual in question. For instance, the grammatical rules of arithmetic could not be appealed to in order to conclusively defeat a doubt about the truth of an arithmetic calculation. That is, each case of doubt about an arithmetic calculation which troubles each philosopher has to be dealt with individually and has its own specific grammatical rules which are of relative concern to that philosophical puzzlement. Further insight into Wittgenstein's therapeutic conception of philosophy can be gained by considering the distinction between changing grammatical rules and altering how grammatical rules are tabulated. (Alternatively put, there are different grammatical rules and different ways of classifying these rules.) Wittgenstein thought that philosophical therapy can work by persuading a philosopher to see the consequences of a commitment drawn from grammatical rules although the grammatical rules themselves remain the same. For example, a philosopher may continue to assert that 'My pain cannot be in the teapot' but be dissuaded from holding that this is a metaphysical truth about pain. In this case, therapy has succeeded by removing a misleading idea about how psychological words are used.

METHODOLOGIES

It is clear that Wittgenstein thought that problems in philosophy can only be tackled by understanding how language is employed and the ways in which philosophers misuse it. Theories in philosophy do not augment the employment of ordinary words but generally solely succeed in using them incorrectly. The apparent plausibility, informative quality, and paradoxical elements of most philosophical theories are not be attributed to any noteworthy information garnered by philosophers but rather to the misuse of language. Wittgenstein stressed that philosophical problems have a variety of causes. He detected a number of types of sources of philosophical confusion. A major one is analogies in the surface grammar of expressions which are actually logically distinct. Wittgenstein remarked that difficulties were created by 'Misunderstandings concerning the use of words, caused, among other things, by certain analogies between the forms of expression in different regions of language' (*PI*, §90). He noted that a root of philosophical problems is misleading analogies in the kind of grammar which is of interest to the linguist. For example, a superficial inspection suggests that 'speaking' and 'meaning' have similar grammars but closer analysis reveals substantial differences between them. Another case is that the affinities between the sentences 'I will keep it in mind' and 'I will keep it in a box' can prompt the thought that the mind is something like a box containing mental content. The nature of this box and its mental contents may then seem mysterious. A related kind of instance is that of not noticing differences of detail in the use of words which can be grouped together (*Z*, §§484f.). However, this invocation of surface grammar as the cause of philosophical problems raises the vexed question of how the phrases 'surface grammar' and 'depth grammar' which occur in the *Investigations* (§664) should be understood. Since no clear explanation of their meaning is given there is controversy over their interpretation. The usual construal of surface grammar is that it is concerned with sentence construction and signifies the rules of grammar which impose restrictions on the combinatorial possibilities of words in producing sentences. Surface grammar is deemed to consist of the obvious syntactic features of sentences and the words which comprise them. In contrast, depth grammar is regarded as controlling the combinatorial possibilities of words in creating meaningful sentences and thereby preventing the creation of nonsensical ones. Another principal generator of philosophical confusion is a failure to realize that certain words are now being used in new ways. A common way in which this happens is that a conceptual innovation is presented as or appears to be a new discovery, but what is actually happening is that new grammatical rules are being introduced. For example, Wittgenstein remarked that in the case of the expression 'unconscious toothache' one 'may either be misled into thinking a stupendous discovery has been made, a discovery which in a sense altogether bewilders our understanding; or else you may be extremely puzzled by the expression (the puzzlement of philosophy)' (*BB*, p. 23). Another instance, is that Freud altered the meaning of the words 'interpretation', 'wish', and 'belief' by employing them in his account of the unconscious. The grammar of the verb 'to wish' was altered by the inclusion of wishes which did not have a conscious expression. A different source of philosophical puzzlement is that stemming from an association of well-known words with particular feelings and thereby incorrectly concluding that such feelings constitute the meanings of those words (*PI*, pp. 174–6 and 181–3). Wittgenstein thought that problems in philosophy arise from a preoccupation with the definitions of and the precise meaning of words. He stated that philosophical confusion arises from thinking that there is a single exact use of a word and finding that the attempt to apply this usage consistently is unsatisfactory because there are instances of the ordinary usage of the word which it does not fit. He claimed that this confusion is dissolved by the recognition that most words are not employed according to precise rules and that this is not a deficiency of ordinary language. Another mistaken tendency is to consider only one sort of example (*PI*, §593). Wittgenstein thought that the 'craving for generality' (*BB*, pp. 17f.) was a primary cause of philosophical problems and that it must be resisted. For example, this craving encourages philosophers to seek precise definitions for family resemblance words such as 'language'. Difficulty arises from the erroneous desire for philosophy to emulate science its in objectives and methods. If philosophy is thought to be the most general of the sciences there will be a strong temptation to resolve philosophical problems through explanatory theories. For instance, Cartesian dualism cannot be refuted by scientific inquiry but only dissolved through clarification of its errors. Philosophical problems are also created by the inclination to push inquiry beyond its legitimate limits because these are not recognized (*Z*, §314, *RFM*, pp. 102f. and *RPPI*, §889). Beyond a certain point the desire to question leads into confusion. Further potent sources of philosophical errors are the projection of the features of one language game on to another and the persuasive power of pictures which are entrenched in language. A case of the latter is that much talk about the mental contains embedded pictures about what must be taking place inside one's mind.

Wittgenstein stressed that there 'is not *a* philosophical method, though there are indeed methods, like different therapies' (*PI*, §133). It is useful to consider some of the methods which he typically employed to resolve philosophical problems. A characteristic of these methods was that he rarely directly challenged a philosophical position and instead favoured more indirect methods of criticism. The reason for this was that Wittgenstein thought that the attraction of a particular philosophical view will not be removed by a careful investigation of its major theoretical expressions. Since the reasons for the attractiveness and compelling power of a position lie deeper than its theoretical expressions it follows that successful criticism of a particular view will only produce new arguments defending it. Instead Wittgenstein thought that philosophical progress could be achieved by questioning the basic and frequently implicit pictures which underpin many philosophical theories. For instance, he thought that the linguistic philosophy of Frege, Russell and the *Tractatus* was underpinned by the Augustinian picture of language and criticized these views through an attack on this picture. Another case was that Wittgenstein's general approach to handling solipsism was to claim that solipsism was mistaking grammatical rules for metaphysical assertions. A fundamental tenet of his philosophical methodology was that once a mistake had been identified it should be returned to repeatedly from a variety of different perspectives so that evermore mistaken assumptions were exposed. This methodological precept was closely linked to Wittgenstein's view that the real resolution of a philosophical problem frequently appears to be a precursor to it.

Wittgenstein also employed more specific methods of combating philosophical error and many of these are the counterparts of typical causes of this. A significant method is that misleading analogies in the surface grammar of expressions which are actually logically distinct can be tackled by descriptions of those particular employments of language which show well-known differences that have escaped notice. These divergences are exhibited in the grammatical explanations of words as these indicate the distinctions between sensible and nonsensical usages of words. For instance, a sentence, such as 'He has toothache but the place where it hurts moves randomly around his body', violates the grammar of the word 'toothache'. Such explanations contribute to Wittgenstein's stated aim of teaching one to 'pass from a piece of disguised nonsense to something that is patent nonsense' (*PI*, §464). Wittgenstein also attempted to dispel misleading analogies in surface grammar by the invention of language games and new employments of words. He thought that the comparison of ordinary usage with these inventions could loosen the deceptive hold of customary linguistic forms (*BB*, p. 28). A technique to counteract the confusion produced by a failure to realize that certain words are now being used in new ways is make the links between apparent conceptual innovations and metaphysical propositions, and the rules of grammar manifest. Wittgenstein thought that typically many propositions of metaphysics hide rules of grammar (*BB*, p. 55). For example, employing the expression 'unknowable pain' may create a metaphysical problem about what might constitute justification for knowing about being in pain. The difficulty is dissolved by the recognition that what is really at issue is the introduction of different grammatical rules. Another method which Wittgenstein employed to combat philosophical mistakes was to enjoin philosophers to devote their attention to particular cases rather than generalizations as these could be misleading. He thought that the problematic tendency to search for definitions which provided the necessary and sufficient conditions for applying a word could be countered by insisting that the actual details of language should be carefully described. Such inspection of language might reveal that an apparent conceptual unity was really a case of family resemblance. Wittgenstein was well aware that certain kinds of linguistic expression appear to conceptualize the structure of reality and argued that this temptation should be resisted by considering the origin and usual usage of these expressions. Akin to this difficulties arising from a problematic expression could be eased by describing how this expression could ordinarily be employed. Wittgenstein claimed that when a method of representing something appears to mirror the very way that reality actually is it should be recalled that the very general facts of nature could have been different with the consequence that certain concepts would have become pointless. When the persuasive power of pictures which are entrenched in language creates confusion, attention should not be focused upon the pictures themselves but on their applications. Wittgenstein discussed particular kinds of temptation to think in mistaken ways and offered suggestions for reducing their appeal. For example, when confronted with a philosophical difficulty there is a propensity to suppose that postulating a mental mechanism would assist in its resolution. He argued that it was helpful to substitute this mental mechanism for a physical one as it would then become clear how little had been achieved by invoking the mind. In a similar fashion against the wish to cast the meaning and understanding of words in terms of mental states which accompany these words, Wittgenstein recommended concentrating upon the actual use of a word. In such cases the irrelevance of mental states to the meaning of words starts to become apparent.

Wittgenstein thought that philosophical problems can only be dissolved or 'explained away' by producing perspicuous representations which show the grammatical confusions that underlie these difficulties (*PI*, §122). The requirement to exhibit these confusions helps to show why a significant tenet of his philosophical methodology was that once a mistake had been identified it should be returned to repeatedly from a variety of different angles. A perspicuous representation is any way in which the similarities and differences between the uses of words in a language is shown. The goal of a perspicuous representation is to show the rules which govern appropriate employments of words. Wittgenstein's investigation is one that tries to achieve a comprehensive overview of a part of language by a perspicuous representation of it rather than aiming to expose all the minutiae of language (*Z*, §§464f.). It is important to be clear about the difference between grammatical rules not being hidden and actually being perspicuous. Grammatical rules are followed by competent speakers of a language and they are open to inspection. As such there is nothing to discover about the rules of grammar but they are not perspicuous (*PR*, §1 and *PI*, §122). For example, Wittgenstein stated that 'An octahedron with the pure colours at the corner-points e.g. provides a *rough* representation of colour-space, and this is a grammatical representation, not a psychological one' (*PR*, §1). He thought that the octahedron was a perspicuous way of expressing the grammar of colour words. Given that there was nothing to discover about grammar it was a necessary feature of language that a perspicuous representation of its grammar can be produced. In principle a survey or map of any segment of language can be created regardless of its size. For instance, a perspicuous representation of the employments of psychological words would be extensive and complex. A perspicuous representation enables a clear view of the usage of any word or group of words to be obtained.

There is dispute over the most suitable interpretation of Wittgenstein's concept of a perspicuous representation. The bird's-eye view model of the employment of the expression 'perspicuous representation' is the predominant one in the specialist literature about this. This model has a number of significant features. One is that it would be mistaken to term classification schemes in general as 'perspicuous representations' since this would not elucidate Wittgenstein's usage of this expression in his discussions of his philosophical methodology. It would also be irrelevant since a perspicuous representation is always of grammar. Such a representation is an ordering or arrangement of grammatical rules or descriptions of word use. A perspicuous representation is produced by the clarification and classification of the grammar of words. That which it represents consists precisely of the grammar described by its various constituent elements. The term 'perspicuous' in 'perspicuous representation' has an attributive usage because it indicates that a certain arrangement of grammatical rules has certain features. These features are that the arrangement can be taken in from a quick inspection, remembered without difficulty, and reproduced with very few errors. A perspicuous representation cannot be more or less perspicuous as an arrangement of grammatical rules which does not have these features is just not a perspicuous representation. In a similar way a representation of grammar cannot be more or less perspicuous than another. (These last two features may possibly be illuminated by a comparison with mathematics. A proof in which the steps do not follow logically is not a proof.)

In the course of philosophical therapy grammatical rules are elicited from an individual. An order in the understanding of language which is related to the dissolution of particular philosophical problems is established by a perspicuous representation (*PI*, §132). The same grammatical rules can be articulated in different ways. However, there is no such thing as having a particular outlook upon the rules of grammar. This is because if there were divergent perspicuous representations of a single segment of grammar any difference would consist in the choice and arrangement of those rules. This difference would be one in how the knowledge of the employment of language was ordered. Perspicuous representations resemble geographical maps in that they can be added together to create a larger representation (or map). The descriptions of grammar which they represent may be merged into a more extensive whole. However, perspicuous representations differ from maps in that a combination of two descriptions of grammar which can both individually be surveyed may become too large to be taken in by a quick inspection. In such a case the perspicuity of the perspicuous representation could only be recovered by further simplification or classification. Perspicuous representations do not have determinate identity criteria such that it is invariably clear whether something does or does not count as one. For example, a fragmentary description of grammar might not in itself meet the requirements for being one. It is possible that a part of a perspicuous representation may cease to be sufficiently complete to be regarded as one and any particular arrangement of grammatical rules may be encompassed by one which is yet wider. It follows from these considerations that there is no way to discover exactly how many perspicuous representations, for example, the *Philosophical Investigations* contains. In a similar way there are no determinate guidelines for ascertaining whether a particular perspicuous representation is successful or adequate. A minimum is clearly that each individual rule of grammar must be correct but beyond that the entire collection must possess a certain level of comprehensiveness or completeness. Indeed it might be thought that the notion of perspicuous representation has a considerable number of the attributes of an essentially contested concept.

There are a number of major differences between the bird's-eye view model and an alternative notion of perspicuous representation (Baker, 2004, pp. 42f.) which focuses upon its connection with seeing aspects of the use of words. In this latter account perspicuous representations do not claim to be correct orderings of the rules of grammar but rather to highlight facets of the employment of words. Whether a perspicuous representation is perspicuous does not depend upon whether it has a number of intrinsic features, such as being taken in from a quick inspection, but is instead a characterization of its role. That is to say a perspicuous representation is no more and no less than a representation which makes perspicuous what is represented. In such a representation the therapeutic value of seeing new aspects is more significant than that of a sharp and unequivocal attempt to demarcate sense from nonsense. Perspicuous representations seek to eliminate the influence of particular unsettling facets of grammar with the aim of allaying philosophical worry. The guidelines for determining whether a particular perspicuous representation is successful are strictly related to particular situations. The extent to which particular philosophical puzzlement is removed in an individual is the measure for assessing their adequacy. In this alternative model of perspicuous representation the idea that Wittgenstein stressed the distinction between descriptions of and pictures of grammar with the aim of elucidating the difference between conceptual analysis and perspicuous representations is important. Allied with this model is stress upon the idea that there is substantial variety in descriptions of grammar and such descriptions may encompass similes, analogies and metaphors. The activity of describing grammar is not routine but one which requires skill and refined judgement about what is appropriate. Just as descriptions of grammar vary significantly so do the guidelines for correct descriptions of it. In the case of pictures of grammar this alternative model of perspicuous representation claims that a fundamental feature of Wittgenstein's philosophical methodology was that there should be negotiation over these pictures. A major point of the distinction between descriptions of and pictures of grammar is that in a perspicuous representation pictures and analogies have priority over the actual description of certain facets of grammar. Given this alternative model several features of his work which would not normally be regarded as perspicuous representations are deemed to be such. For example, some of Wittgenstein's best-known philosophical slogans should not be viewed as stating facts of grammar but as perspicuous representations which are analogical in character whose aim is to persuade one to see things in a different way. A case of this is that his slogan 'thinking is operating with signs' should not be regarded as supplying information about the grammar of the word 'thinking'. Instead its role is to persuade an individual suffering from philosophical puzzlement about the character of thinking to acknowledge particular personal grammatical prejudices that create this confusion.

SCOPE OF PHILOSOPHICAL THERAPY

Wittgenstein's influence has declined in the last 25 years or so against a widespread acceptance of the continuity between philosophy and science. Arguably this trend at least partially stems from the work of Quine and his influence in promoting new sorts of linguistic philosophy. Such movements have been complemented by developments in theoretical linguistics by Chomsky and his followers. The picture offered here is that problems of how linguistic creativity is possible are tackled by the creation of a theory of meaning for language. Scientific investigations aided by philosophical analysis will demonstrate that language is a complex system of rules that are tacitly known to speakers. Another significant trend is that the rise of the computer has encouraged the construal of the operations of the mind and brain on a functionalist model. Advances in neuroscience have promoted attempts to combine linguistics, artificial intelligence, psychology and the philosophies of language and mind with the resulting emergence of the field of cognitive science. These recent historical developments raise the issue of whether Wittgenstein's declining influence reflects an appropriate assessment of the value of his philosophical methodology or rather a failure to understand the full significance of his approach. Views about Wittgenstein's methodology range between regarding it as the solution to all philosophical problems and as of very little value. The fields to which his approach has been applied include the philosophies of language, logic, mind, cognitive science, mathematics, religion, aesthetics, ethics, political and social philosophy and jurisprudence. It is widely accepted that his methodology varies in its effectiveness in different areas of philosophy. A central question is whether the variable effectiveness is caused by some failing in the method itself which manifests itself more sharply in some philosophical fields than others or by differences between philosophical areas or indeed by some combination of these factors. Serious reflection on this matter should lead to a more nuanced approach to the significance of Wittgenstein's philosophy.

The limitations of Wittgenstein's philosophical methodology should be recognized. The issue is whether there are inherent restrictions upon the applicability of the methodology caused by shortcomings within it. Criticisms of it provide insight into the identification of these limitations. There are a number of major types of objection to Wittgenstein's methodology. Probably the feature which has provoked the most controversy is the idea that there is no theoretical element in philosophy. Traditionally philosophy was conceived as the most general of the sciences. A common objection to Wittgenstein's approach is that it radically decreases (or eliminates) the challenge and interest of philosophy. A way of countering this criticism is to recognize the sources of philosophical difficulty. Philosophy is as complex as the confusions in thinking that it unravels. Emergence from confusion can be a lengthy and intricate process. The depth of philosophical problems arises from their being rooted in the ways of human thought and such similar difficulties with different manifestations will continue to reappear. Another major criticism of Wittgenstein's view that philosophy does not contain a theoretical component is that all philosophical distinctions are grounded in some kind of theoretical framework. A response to this is that for Wittgenstein any deeper explanation would just be a further grammatical rule which stands in the same relation to linguistic usage as the rules that it supposedly explains. There are no explanatory or argumentative hierarchies in philosophy. The context of reference for his inquiries was shaped by their grammatical content but it was not part of a theoretical framework he was propounding. Wittgenstein's position that there are no theses in philosophy other than trivial ones which no one would disagree with (*PI*, §128) has been criticized on the grounds that it is inadequately justified and the weakest aspect of his thought. It has been claimed that Wittgenstein's actual practice is inconsistent with his professed repudiation of philosophical theses because theses which he proffered can be formulated. In support of this criticism it is argued that since philosophical theses are not supposed to be present in his work they appear in a piecemeal impromptu fashion and are sometimes not argued for. For example, some commentators interpret Wittgenstein's claim that meaning is used as a commitment to antirealist semantic theory which replaced truth conditions with assertion conditions even though he disavowed philosophical theories. It is clearly possible to produce what appear to be philosophical claims which are attributable to Wittgenstein. The strength of this objection depends whether these claims are regarded as such or taken as being grammatical remarks aimed at philosophical therapy. Another aspect of the criticism that his actual practice and avowed rejection of philosophical theories were inconsistent is whether it appears to apply to some parts of Wittgenstein's work more than others. For instance, a particular troubling case is his practice in the philosophy of mathematics where there seem to be a number of substantive claims about legitimate methods and constructions. A criticism of Wittgenstein's methodology is that it prevents the systematic pursuit of philosophy. He thought that a comprehensive treatment of grammar was possible but that this was frequently irrelevant to the pursuit of philosophical inquiry. Philosophy does not seek to generate a grammar as such but is concerned with grammar in order to resolve philosophical difficulty. The perspicuous representations which philosophy seeks to produce are systematic although not comprehensive (as each one represents a part of grammar).

Wittgenstein claimed that appropriate descriptions resolve philosophical problems by showing how they are created by linguistic abuses and that what is required is a description of the uses of language. Since grammar is arbitrary the linguistic community's grammatical rules cannot be correct or accord truthfully with the facts. Grammatical rules are in themselves neither correct nor incorrect. They distinguish correct from incorrect linguistic usage and it is possible for them to be altered (or alternatively put a community of language users can change the way that they talk). There is no standard of correctness for use of language over and beyond this. It has been objected that this is an inadequate norm of correctness but this objection is effectively one to Wittgenstein's position that grammar is arbitrary. A different kind of critique is that his methodology is unsatisfactory because resolving linguistic confusions in the language of one's community cannot take place within this language and must occur within a meta-language (which is used to describe this language). In contrast to this, Wittgenstein claimed that any explanation in a meta-language would simply be another rule of grammar which stands in the same relation to linguistic usage as the rules that it supposedly explains. Another criticism of Wittgenstein's philosophical methodology which is related to standards of correctness for the employment of language is that it favours descriptions of existing usage over proposed revisions to this. This bias can produce misleading conclusions about the nature of reality. An illustration of this objection is that according to existing grammatical rules it is nonsense to claim that a patch of colour is reddish green. However, a psychological experiment indicates that people do actually see a coloured patch as reddish green. In this case attention to the grammatical rules would lead to a mistaken claim about the nature of perception. A response to this is that Wittgenstein's idea that grammar is arbitrary has the consequence that how the grammatical rules conceptualize reality is arbitrary in that the community's particular conceptualization cannot be said to be more or less correct or justified than some other partitioning of reality that could have been adopted. However, there can be factors, such as the nature of human interests, which incline the linguistic community to alter the grammatical rules that are adhered to. In the example, the experiment could be taken into consideration and the rules changed so that it makes sense to say that a patch of colour is reddish green. A related kind of critique is that Wittgenstein's favouring descriptions of existing usage over proposed revisions to language hinders the construction of new theories which involve alterations to current linguistic practices. He would have thought that the very motivation for this objection was misguided as philosophy does not contain a theoretical component. Wittgenstein's philosophical methodology has been questioned on the grounds that philosophical work consists of more than just descriptions of grammar and their employment in dissolving problems. A corollary to this criticism is that detailed inspection of the employment of language may establish distinctions and links that may be insufficiently general and extensive for full philosophical understanding. However, it might be thought that a successful perspicuous representation is of interest in virtue of the descriptive illumination it offers and independently of its role in the resolution of philosophical problems. The objection about what philosophical activity comprises is a fundamental one and the attitude taken towards it reflects one's overall estimation of the value of Wittgenstein's work. As Wittgenstein himself stressed the worth of his methodology was to be judged by its results.

An issue is whether the variable effectiveness of Wittgenstein's methodology is related to different philosophical fields requiring distinct methodological approaches. It is useful to determine the areas where his methodology seems most profitable and the reasons for this. The question of whether Wittgenstein's actual practice is inconsistent with his professed repudiation of philosophical theses has a bearing on the matter of the areas in which his methodology seems to be most valuable. If he was inconsistent then it is possible that his philosophical methodology might appear to work better in certain areas than it actually should because his practice of philosophical analysis in these fields involves making some substantive claims despite his professions to the contrary. Wittgenstein's methodology appears to be most effective for the philosophies of language and mind. His descriptive method is suited to the area of the philosophy of mind as mental phenomena exhibit a huge and subtle range of variation. It seems to work less well for the philosophy of mathematics. It looks as though it operates least satisfactorily in the fields of aesthetics, ethics, political and social philosophy and jurisprudence. The relative lack of success in these fields is probably linked to the fact that Wittgenstein wrote very little on aesthetics, almost nothing on ethics after 1929 and never on political and social philosophy or jurisprudence. It might be thought that Wittgenstein's methodological recommendation that philosophical work consists of descriptions of grammar and their employment in dissolving problems is inappropriate for aesthetics, ethics, political and social philosophy and jurisprudence. This is because it could be claimed that these areas are distinctively different from those which were at the forefront of Wittgenstein's interest. It is neither appropriate nor possible to argue either for or against this view here but an outline of what is at stake can be given. In contrast to areas like the philosophy of language or epistemology in the fields of aesthetics, ethics, political and social philosophy and jurisprudence the task of philosophy is to shape the meanings of difficult or unclear expressions. A good many expressions in these fields are ones whose meaning needs elucidation and whose links with other expressions requires clarification. It is hard to see how the precepts of Wittgenstein's philosophical methodology should be expanded to cover these areas and also whether they should be expanded without modification. Insight into why the application of his methodology to these particular philosophical fields is problematic can be gained through consideration of the idea that the role of philosophy here is to make intuitions about concepts and their connections explicit. These notions may be related in ways which are either unclear or problematic and there may turn out to be gaps in the connections between them. Indeed such concepts may have little or no systematic framework or method of organization. Given this a philosophical methodology which simply scrutinizes the usage of these expressions, such as 'beautiful', will not in itself dissolve philosophical confusion about the nature of the associated concept, such as beauty. It follows from this that philosophical activity should aim to clarify the relations between and fill in any lacunae in the current employment of such expressions. However, their existing usage should not be altered because doing so would change the conceptual relationships. Progress should be made by consulting conceptual intuitions about the expressions in question with the objective of elucidating how and why the present rules for their employment can be profitably expanded. The success of this elucidation is to be judged by the extent to which it illuminates the philosophical problems under consideration.

CHAPTER 6

PHILOSOPHY OF LANGUAGE
AND MATHEMATICS

GRAMMAR AND MEANING

Concerns about language fundamentally shape the *Investigations*. The book begins with a quote from Augustine's *Confessions* which 'give us a particular picture of the essence of human language' (*PI*, §1). This picture is based on the idea that words are the names of objects and the meaning of each one is the object which it stands for. The connection between words and their meanings is established by ostensive definition and this form of definition is the foundation of language. Words are mentally associated with objects (*PI*, §32) which has the consequence that learning the public language of the linguistic community is only possible if an individual already has a private language.[1] Sentences are combinations of names (*PI*, §1). Understanding the meaning of a sentence is knowing what is described by it. This knowledge arises from comprehending what the words stand for and how they are combined (*PI*, §§21–7). Wittgenstein thought that the Augustinian picture idea that all language is descriptive does not adequately account for the whole range and complexity of linguistic practices. It follows that picture cannot be relied upon as a basis for developing linguistic theories which apply to language in its entirety. The language game in which a builder and his assistant use four words (block, pillar, slab, beam) describes a language which is correctly characterized by the Augustinian picture (*PI*, §2).[2] This clearly indicates the severe limitations of the picture. Wittgenstein thought that the linguistic philosophy of Frege, Russell and the *Tractatus* was underpinned by the Augustinian picture of language and criticized these views through an attack on this picture. Much of the *Investigations* is devoted to criticism of the picture and the development of alternative ways of looking at and understanding language. The aim of the discussion of Wittgenstein's philosophy of language is to elucidate certain fundamental conceptions which shaped his thinking. A better comprehension of these enables one to appreciate the place which notions like family resemblance have in his work.

The concept of grammar played a central role in Wittgenstein's philosophy as a whole. A useful starting point for his idea of grammar is to consider what he took the notion to cover. There are different concepts of grammar. Traditional descriptive grammar of linguists describes the normative regularities of a language and concentrates upon syntax. It aims to investigate linguistic organization and structure. The concerns of traditional descriptive grammar include the parts of speech (such as nouns and adverbs), arranging declensions, tense formation, regularities in verb conjugation, and the like. It also deals with the classification of sentences into different forms, and the relations between these forms (such as the transformation of positive imperatives into the corresponding negative ones). Traditional descriptive grammar is what the concept of grammar is ordinarily taken to be. It seems that the scope of Wittgenstein's usage of the idea of grammar remained the same from the middle to the late period. His employment of the word 'grammar' was unusual, complex and considerably wider than, but related to, the ordinary use of the word. This is because Wittgenstein's concept of grammar encompassed many phenomena which are ordinarily not regarded as grammatical at all, such as any sort of explanations of meaning, category distinctions and mathematical propositions. He readily acknowledged this in his writings (see for example *PR*, §1).

Wittgenstein claimed that grammatical rules (*PG*, §133) are arbitrary and repudiated the *Tractatus'* idea that language reflects metaphysics. Grammar is not arbitrary in that it is either unimportant or a question of personal preferences. The sense in which grammar is arbitrary is that the linguistic community's grammatical rules cannot be correct or accord truthfully with the facts. What the linguistic community says accords with the facts if it is true but the truths are not themselves grammatical rules. For instance, a system of measurement is neither correct or incorrect in the way that a statement of weight is. How a linguistic community's grammatical rules partition or conceptualize reality is arbitrary in that the community's particular conceptualization cannot be said to be 'right', 'true', 'justified', or 'better justified' and so on, than some other partitioning of reality that could have been adopted. For example, grammatical rules which provide transitions between different uses of words can be invented (*PI*, §122) to provide illustrations of this point. Some consequences of grammar being arbitrary are that there is no *a priori* justification for grammatical rules taking the form that they do and that grammatical rules do not have any metaphysical component or significance. An example which shows some of these points is the arbitrariness of the colour system, that is, the grammatical rules governing colour words. It cannot be asserted that the linguistic community's colour system, which rules out phrases such as 'bluish orange', is more correct than a system which permits it. Wittgenstein's insistence on the arbitrariness of grammar should not be taken to imply that the nature of human interests and the nature of reality have no bearing at all upon what the linguistic community's grammatical rules are. There are factors which incline the adoption of particular grammatical rules rather than others and from this point of view grammar is not arbitrary. For instance, Wittgenstein (*Z*, §§357f.) commented that there was something about the colour system which is simultaneously both arbitrary and non-arbitrary. The grammar of colour words does not lie in the properties of colours because grammar is arbitrary. Rather, the notion of colour is produced by the grammatical rules for the use of colour words. However, for reasons which are connected to what fixes which concepts the linguistic community forms (such as the very general facts of nature) the colour system is non-arbitrary. Some things, for example that people see in colour and insects do not, speak in favour of one representation rather than another.

Wittgenstein thought that grammatical rules cannot be judged against reality because these rules differentiate sense from nonsense. They distinguish correct from incorrect linguistic usage. As grammatical rules are arbitrary they are in themselves neither correct nor incorrect (*PR*, §4). It is possible for the rules of grammar to be altered (or alternatively put a community of language users can change the way that they talk). Wittgenstein's view was that nonsense is nonsense because it has not been admitted into the language as making sense. For example, a sentence which he regarded as nonsensical was that 'a colour is a semitone higher than another'. The grammatical conventions (which is another way of talking about grammatical rules) exclude the statement that colours have sounds (and the like) but the rules could be changed. The sentence cannot be proved to be nonsense since if the meanings of the words were understood differently it could be made sense of (*PR*, §4).

There is no substantive consensus about whether the rules for distinguishing sense from nonsense belong to syntax or semantics. What the parameters of syntax are taken to be and the degree to which syntax and semantics are regarded as separable varies considerably. The various concepts of syntax and semantics are a concomitant of the different concepts of grammar. Wittgenstein held that there was no fundamental way of distinguishing between syntax and semantics because both were concerned with the rules of grammar which are arbitrary.[3] He extended the scope of the notion of grammar beyond that of traditional descriptive grammar as he regarded it as comprising what comes under syntax and semantics. For example, Wittgenstein remarked that the 'part of speech is only determined by *all* the grammatical rules which hold for a word and seen from this point of view our language contains countless different parts of speech' (*PR*, §92). This is an alternative characterization of the familiar notion of a part of speech where different syntactic and semantic grammatical rules hold for distinct parts of speech. A consequence of this is that it is unacceptable for one part of speech to be substituted for another. From this perspective the traditional descriptive grammar method of analysing a language by examining syntactic forms does not accord sufficient weight to the role which semantics plays in grammar. Another case is that Wittgenstein thought grammar had categories (*PG*, §76 and *PI*, §97). However, these are not sharply delineated because the sort of words which fall under a grammatical category cannot always be substituted for one another without any change of significance. Syntax and semantics cannot be precisely distinguished when considering what constitutes categorial sense and nonsense.

A rough characterization of pragmatics is that it covers the employment and effects of linguistic entities, such as words, within the behavioural circumstances of their occurrence. Traditional descriptive grammar excludes pragmatics from the concept of grammar. There is no major agreement about what the notions of semantics and pragmatics should properly encompass. The different concepts of semantics and pragmatics are a concomitant of the diverse concepts of grammar. Wittgenstein disputed the clear separation of semantics from pragmatics. He expanded the range of the concept of grammar as he thought it included aspects of pragmatics.

A facet of Wittgenstein's view that there was no clear boundary between semantics and pragmatics was his claim that the meaningfulness of a sentence is not solely determined by syntactic and semantic considerations. He thought that whether or not a sentence is meaningful is frequently dependent upon the circumstances of its utterance (*BB*, pp. 9ff.). Wittgenstein disagreed with the position that a sentence can be understood and yet its function remains entirely obscure. The employment of a sentence may require an explanation which has not yet been given. Wittgenstein's point about what a fully adequate characterization of meaningfulness consists in applies to more linguistic phenomena and issues than just sentences. An important extension of this is that the distinction between sense and nonsense characteristically depends upon circumstances (*AWL*, pp. 20f.). There is not a single invariant concept of sense (or nonsense) which is governed by the rules of syntax and semantics and is entirely circumstance independent. The corollary to this is that what counts as nonsense can be variously characterized depending upon the circumstances of the sentence. It follows that there are as many different ideas of nonsense as there are reasons in different circumstances for asserting that some expression is nonsensical. On Wittgenstein's view it is not possible to argue that there is a best reason for regarding a sentence as nonsensical.

The *Investigations* focuses upon the related themes of meaning, explanation of meaning and understanding. Wittgenstein stressed the connection between the use and meaning of language. He remarked (*PI*, §43): 'For a *large* class of cases – though not for all – in which we employ the word "meaning" it can be defined thus: the meaning of a word is its use in the language'. Wittgenstein was not offering a general theory that the meaning of a word is its use but was rather drawing attention to an important feature of our linguistic practice. He employed his ideas about meaning to focus attention upon the community's ordinary linguistic practices and thereby to assist in the dissolution of the puzzling theoretical questions about the notion of meaning. Wittgenstein remarked (*PG*, §32): 'But we said that by "meaning" we meant what an explanation of meaning explains'. This quote and close paraphrases of it, such as meaning is that which is explained in providing an explanation of meaning, need to be interpreted within the framework of Wittgenstein's general treatment of meaning for their importance to become clear. As the rules of grammar which differentiate between sense and nonsense include any rules for the correct use of words and explanations of meaning are rules for employing words correctly it is the case that every explanation of the meaning of a word belongs to grammar. Providing an explanation of meaning consists in showing some of the links in the network of connected grammatical rules. For example, explaining the meaning of the word 'number' would provide rules for assessing the correct use of numerical expressions. One of these rules is that sounds cannot be ascribed to numbers. There is no metaphysics underpinning explanations of meaning which must be discovered or elucidated because grammar is arbitrary. If this is taken in conjunction with Wittgenstein's view that meaning is what is explained by an explanation of meaning (*PI*, §560) it follows that meaning does not have a metaphysical component. He was concerned with how language is taught as part of his investigation into meaning. Wittgenstein claimed that he was 'making a connexion between the concept of teaching and the concept of meaning' (*Z*, §412). One of his observations was that the way of teaching the meaning of a word is to supply an explanation of the meaning of the word.

Wittgenstein thought that the meaning of a word is not something more profound and theoretically complex than what is evident in the normal practice of explaining the word. He emphasized that the practice of explanation is one which is well known to the speakers of the language and accessible to scrutiny. Wittgenstein maintained that the examination of explanations is the usual way for establishing truths about the meaning of words. For instance, an explanation of the meaning of the word 'cricket' is that it is a popular summer team sport which is played with a bat and ball. Other examples of explanations of the meaning of 'cricket' could be those of paraphrasing a description of the game from a book on the sport, or pointing to a game of cricket on the television. These are just accepted explanations of the meaning of the word 'cricket'; no more and no less. However, the meaning of cricket is not explained by saying that it is something which is ultimately comprised of sub-atomic particles or a game in which the motion of the ball obeys the laws of physics. These are not acceptable explanations but they could be if the usual practices of explaining the word changed. Wittgenstein contended that community consensus about acceptable practices of explanation is sufficient to distinguish correct from incorrect explanations. It was central to his conception of explanations of meaning that all forms of explanation of meaning are adequate. Wittgenstein stressed that diverse explanations of the same word can be equally acceptable. He thought that there was considerable diversity in the kinds of explanation of meaning, as these ranged from ostensive definition to explanation by paraphrase and explanation through examples. For instance, Wittgenstein remarked that ostensive explanations of meaning can be provided for proper names, the names of colours, and the like (*PI*, §28). A case of explaining meaning by paraphrase is that of 'peculiar' standing 'for some such expression as "out of the ordinary" ' (*BB*, p. 158). From traditional philosophy of language perspectives this variety of explanations of meaning raises the issue of whether these really are adequate explanations of meaning. Wittgenstein argued that the linguistic community's ordinary explanations of meaning are adequate: what we want to know about meaning is provided by them. Concentrating upon these explanations is philosophically enlightening. Wittgenstein claimed that maintaining that meaning can be explained in a variety of ways helps to highlight the need for the philosopher to pay attention to the community's ordinary linguistic practices when he is troubled by questions about meaning (*BB*, p. 1 and *PI*, §560).

There is a substantial difference between how explanations of meaning are treated by Wittgenstein, and by many traditional points of view in the philosophy of language. He objected to theories of meaning which postulated (or invoked) the view that the meaning of a word is the object which it stands for. For example, classical sense and reference theories fall into this category. Wittgenstein maintained that metaphysics does not underpin meaning. He devoted considerable attention to criticism of accounts which claimed that the meaning of a word was to be explained as a mental representation of some kind. For instance, one of his objections to this view was that it allows the possibility that each individual could mean something different by a word. Wittgenstein rejected the idea of definition as analysis and its corollaries about ideal explanations of meaning. An explanation of this sort is a definition which provides the necessary and sufficient conditions for applying a word. He cast aspersions on the notion of ideal explanations due to the emphasis on the adequacy of ordinary explanations of meaning. Wittgenstein also repudiated the notion that some kinds of explanations are preferable or true. For example, accounts of natural kind terms which regard science as giving insight into the meaning of words belong to this group. The ordinary language classification of species differs from scientific taxonomy in that it is overwhelmingly anthropocentric. He thought that although one explanation of the meaning of a word is scientifically grounded and the other is not each is just as legitimate as the other. Every theory of meaning which departs from the idea that the meaning of a word is tied to explanations of its meaning differs from Wittgenstein's position. Understanding is connected to meaning and its explanation in the senses that the content of understanding is meaning and explanation is correlated with understanding. Failure to understand an explanation of meaning is manifested in incorrect usage. Understanding is a family resemblance concept but it is most akin to an ability.

RULES AND FORMS OF LIFE

The concepts of rules and rule-following are central to the later philosophy. For instance, they are part of the framework of the private language argument because of questions about whether it is possible to follow a rule privately. The theme of rule-following appeared regularly in Wittgenstein's writings and received significant sustained coverage in the *Investigations*, §§185–242. His treatment of it diverged significantly from major established perspectives. Wittgenstein sought to show that many ostensible problems about rule-following have their roots in misconceptions about what it is to follow a rule. A major target of criticism was the conception that a rule is an abstract entity which transcends all of its particular applications. He thought that a frequent underlying confusion about rule-following concerned how a rule determines its future applications. Part of this difficulty stems from the mistaken idea that if one can naturally draw the consequences of a rule to oneself then all of these consequences must somehow be present in the rule already. For Wittgenstein, a rule is a norm of correctness but such normativity is neither a causal nor general lawlike property. There is a conceptual connection between a rule and that which is deemed to accord with it. The method of application of a rule, which is shown in practice, and how rules are used determines whether there is accord with a rule or not. Rule-following is a command of a technique (possibly involving training) and is usually displayed on a multiplicity of occasions. For example, Wittgenstein investigated the case of teaching a pupil to follow orders of the form '+ n'. He remarked that 'we get the pupil to continue a series (say + 2) beyond 1000 – and he writes 1000, 1004, 1008, 1012' (*PI*, §185). A principal objective for Wittgenstein was to dissolve some of the temptations which prompt the claim that the results of a properly conducted mathematical calculation are the inevitable outcome of the meaning of the formula shaping the values which are written. He thought that a certain mathematical training which teaches the use of a formula, such by getting the pupil to do exercises, ensures that individuals should always write the appropriate values. The pupil's mastery of the series is demonstrated by the technique of applying the rule to produce an appropriate series of numbers. If (as in the example) the pupil writes '1000' and then '1004' then the order '+ 2' has clearly been contravened. The reason for judging that the pupil has failed to understand this order correctly is that the values were incorrect. Wittgenstein investigated the issues which arise from the pupil being corrected and responding with a claim that the series had been continued as meant. He insisted upon the distinction between actually according with a rule and merely believing that one is. Wittgenstein claimed that being in accord with a rule is not determined by whether an individual thinks he is in accord but by actions in practice which accord with it. According with a rule requires a norm of correctness in practice. A significant distinction for Wittgenstein is that between being in accord with and following a rule. To follow a rule an individual must intend to follow it and be able to invoke it in account of his practice if required. For instance, a rule might be cited as an explanation for particular actions. The cases of rule-following which have been considered here are straightforward but there have been substantial attempts (notably in jurisprudence) to extend Wittgenstein's treatment of rule-following to cases where it is difficult to determine whether a rule is being followed or not.

A controversial issue is whether a solitary individual could follow a rule. It should be observed that this is not the matter of whether an individual can follow rules which are particular to himself and unknown to the rest of the linguistic community. Instead the question is whether it is possible for an individual to follow a rule in the absence of a community. This problem is usually cast in terms of a lifelong Crusoe who is characterized as an individual isolated from birth with a language devised for his own purposes but without having first learnt a language from another. The received view is that it is highly doubtful whether a lifelong Crusoe would engage in activities which would appropriately be termed rule-following. Some commentators, such as Baker and Hacker (1985), oppose the standard position in holding that such a lifelong Crusoe could follow his own rules agreeing over time with himself in judgements and behaviour. Even if not psychologically possible it is conceivable that a lifelong Crusoe should employ some kind of language and follow rules in doing so. A contentious and much discussed piece of commentary upon rule-following is Saul Kripke's *Wittgenstein on Rules and Private Language*. Kripke presented his views as arising from Wittgenstein's argument about rule-following as it struck him. He claimed that Wittgenstein was a sceptic about any kind of meaning because he held that any interpretative rule will itself be subject to a variety of interpretations *ad infinitum*. That is to say, no rule can ever be interpreted so as to exclude any possible misinterpretation. Kripke argued that what counts as correct rule-following is not determined by the rule itself but by what the community accepts as following it. For instance, whether '2 + 2 = 4' depends upon what the community and especially its designed experts acknowledges. Correct cannot be defined independently of what this community either accepts or can be persuaded to regard as acceptable. This is a very strong version of the position that it is not possible for an individual to follow a rule in the absence of a community. It is widely agreed by scholars that Kripke's views are dubious as interpretation of Wittgenstein's remarks on rule-following.

Wittgenstein included things which were almost never previously conceived of as rules into the category of rules. In the *Principles of Linguistic Philosophy* Waismann thought that Wittgenstein was recommending a new employment of the word 'rule'. This usage was warranted by the analogies between the phenomena that he regarded as coming under his extended scope of the term 'rule', such as ostensive definitions and arithmetic propositions, and things which would ordinarily be regarded as rules. However, it appears that Wittgenstein was not concerned to alter the employment of the word 'rule' but to show that ostensive definitions, mathematical propositions and so on were actually rules. He claimed that what is used as a rule is a rule. The corollary to this is that some phenomena, such as metaphysical propositions, have the employment of rules although the linguistic community does not term them rules. A better understanding of this point requires a detailed elucidation of the similarities between the employment of such phenomena and things which are uncontroversially called rules. Recognizing these ideas makes Wittgenstein's discussion of the relationship between grammar and necessity easier to understand. In the discussion of grammar earlier in this chapter it was observed that he readily acknowledged that his concept of grammar encompassed many phenomena which are ordinarily not regarded as grammatical at all. Wittgenstein's reasoning for their inclusion in the notion of grammar utilized his idea that what is used as a rule is a rule. He employed this idea to claim that what is used as a grammatical rule is a grammatical rule.

Wittgenstein devoted considerable attention to the relationship between grammar and necessity. He did not approach questions about necessity from the traditional starting point of asking what the origin of necessity is, such as inquiring whether the necessity of logical propositions lies in the world, and thus his handling of necessity differed markedly in perspective from the usual treatments of the notion. Wittgenstein dealt with issues in a radically different way to many existing theories about necessity. His central idea was that what philosophers term necessary propositions are characteristically arbitrary grammatical rules. Wittgenstein remarked (*PI*, §372):

> Consider: 'The only correlate in language to an intrinsic necessity is an arbitrary rule. It is the only thing which one can milk out of this intrinsic necessity into a proposition.'

What is necessary is an arbitrary grammatical rule and any particular rule could have been different. Necessary propositions express relationships between linked concepts. As these propositions are grammatical rules they are not descriptions of any kind and differentiate sense from nonsense. A corollary is that the negation of a necessary proposition is not another kind of proposition, such as an empirical one, but something which is not a proposition at all. This is because the denial of a necessary proposition is a piece of nonsense which has contravened grammatical rules. For example, consider the case of the necessity of the colour system. He commented (*Z*, §331):

> One is tempted to justify rules of grammar by sentences like 'But there really are four primary colours'. And the saying that the rules of grammar are arbitrary is directed against the possibility of this justification, which is constructed on the model of justifying a sentence by pointing to what verifies it.

Wittgenstein held that it is part of the grammar of colour words that there are only four primary colours. He claimed that a colour octahedron was one way of expressing this and other grammatical features of colour words (*PR*, §§1 and 39). A necessary proposition which states that two colour predicates cannot be applied to the same physical space is part of the rules of grammar for colour words. Wittgenstein thought recognizing that apparently necessary propositions are actually expressions of grammatical rules dissolves some of the confusion surrounding the notion of necessary propositions.

Wittgenstein examined the propositions of mathematics, logic and metaphysics with respect to their status as necessary. His general view about these propositions can be illustrated by considering an aspect of it that he regarded as important which is that typically many propositions of metaphysics conceal rules of grammar. Wittgenstein gave a similar account of the formulations of metaphysical impossibilities to that of necessary propositions as he argued that the rules of grammar determined what is deemed to be an impossibility of this kind. Metaphysically impossible propositions are actually (concealed) rules of grammar which demarcate the limits of sense. For example, propositions which state that a patch of colour cannot be both red and green appear to preclude metaphysical impossibilities. From a traditional standpoint the reason why a proposition, such as 'X is green and X is red' (where an object may be substituted for 'X'), is inadmissible is because of the properties of colours (that is, the physics of light). The modal word 'cannot' which suggests a misleading analogy with a physical inability encourages this construal of these sorts of propositions. Wittgenstein claimed that a proposition like 'X is green, so X is not red' seems to be a description of the physical properties of colour (just as the proposition 'Nothing can be processed using uranium without becoming radioactive' is a description of chemical attributes) but it is not. He thought that the apparent proposition about metaphysical impossibility hides grammatical rules which distinguish sense from nonsense in the use of colour words. Wittgenstein argued that the rules of grammar prevent the formation of propositions such as 'X is red and X is green'. He maintained that the proposition is misleading because it is employed as a grammatical rule to linguistically exclude the description of a patch of colour as being both red and green at the same time. The grammatical rule also prevents inferences of the kind 'X is red' and 'X is green' to the proposition 'X is simultaneously red and green' or allows inferences like 'X is green, so X is not red'. If the rule is broken, such as in 'this patch of colour is both red and green', then the result is nonsense. Replacing the modal 'cannot' with 'it is nonsense to say' makes the true nature of supposedly metaphysically impossible propositions clearer.

Wittgenstein was interested in the use of sentences when considering necessity. He thought that the distinction between necessary and contingent propositions is related to their use. The same sentence can be used to state a necessary or contingent proposition and conversely different sentences can have the same employment. Wittgenstein remarked that one should look at a 'sentence as an instrument, and at its sense as its employment' (*PI*, §421). For example, depending upon the particular use the sentence 'Ten plus three is thirteen' may make a necessary proposition about part of the grammar of numbers or it may make a contingent claim about the quantity of objects that there are in a box. Differentiations between necessary and contingent propositions cannot be made without considering the particular uses of sentences.

Wittgenstein considered the non-linguistic context of language. He claimed that a linguistic community must agree in definitions and judgements. Agreement in definitions is accord over the rules of use for words. Agreement in judgements is accord over what counts as the correct applications of a rule. Wittgenstein thought that agreement in judgements (or at minimum in a core of judgements) is a requirement for having agreement in definitions (*PI*, §242). The form of life and the general facts of nature are parts of the framework within which language occurs. The form of life is a much contested area and there is abundant discussion about it. Agreement in form of life is not detachable from agreement in definitions and in judgements. Wittgenstein used the expression 'form(s) of life' a very small number of times. Haller (1988) argues that he employed the phrase in at least two distinct ways. One use is to summarize 'the common human way of acting', that which is particularly and universally human. This refers to the biological aspects of human nature. Another usage is to stress differences between societies. This refers to the cultural aspects of human nature.[4] However, some commentators would disagree with the distinction between the two strands that Haller makes because they would regard the concept of forms of life as fundamentally being about the cultural aspects of human nature. In the case of the cultural features of a form of life Wittgenstein was concerned with cultural practices in a broad way that encompassed both anthropology and sociology. These practices affect various society's agreement in definitions and judgements about particular linguistic usages. An example of cultural practices is the use of the word 'responsibility' in an ancient Greek legal case about a boy who threw a javelin and accidentally killed another boy. It was considered whether the judges of the contest, the person who threw the javelin or the javelin itself was responsible for the accident. What this instance illustrates is that agreement in definitions and judgements about words can vary widely between societies. The biological facets of a form of life are concerned with the very general facts about human biology which are common to the human race as a whole, such as a person having one body. For example, agreement in definitions and in judgements about the word 'joy' are related to joy being an emotion without a stable physical location in the body.

Both strands of form(s) of life rest upon, but are not the same as the very general facts of nature. The very general facts of nature are the background stabilities of the natural world. Wittgenstein stressed that these facts of nature could have been different (*PI*, p. 230). He thought that the very general facts of nature impose limitations upon which concepts are natural or unnatural to nearly all human beings and that these concepts could run along very divergent lines to the usual ones if the general facts of nature had been different (*PI*, p. 230 and *RPPII*, §§706–8). For instance, a human being would find the notion of transferring his emotions to an inanimate object an unnatural demand (*RPPI*, §48). There are practical reasons relating to aspects of human nature which influence concepts. A case of this is that of enormously complex numerals not being used because of the difficulties of manipulating them (*RFM*, p. 73). A concept is formed when a similarity is important to a community (*Z*, §§376–80). For example, pointless concepts such as those for each kind of hair colour a philosopher could have do not arise because they do not reflect natural distinctions.

The very general facts of nature play a part in elucidating the position that the linguistic community's concepts are arbitrary and determined by convention. That is, the community could have decided otherwise. Specific contingent regularities are preconditions for the applicability of particular concepts. If these regularities did not hold the use of certain concepts would not have a point (*PI*, §142, p. 174 and *Z*, §568). For instance, it is a fact about human biology that in general pain has a location in the body which is stable (*Z*, §483). Wittgenstein thought that the idea that the place where pains occurred moved around, such as shifting from a person to an object as in the pain of a tooth is lying on the table (*PR*, §§64f.), or going randomly around in an individual's body (*RPPI*, §440), was problematic. Postulating a change like this in the general facts of nature contravened the framework in which the normal notion of pain location was employed and took away the point of using the concept. Another case is that Wittgenstein (*BB*, pp. 61f.) held that if people had bodies which appeared identical but had different voices the normal concept of personal identity would no longer fulfil the purposes for which it is used. This is because the general facts of nature which form the background to the normal notion have altered. A corollary to this is that the usual rules for the use of these concepts would cease to have a point. For example, a rule for the application of the notion of personal identity such as having a distinct bodily identity would fail to have any useful purpose. Wittgenstein stressed that human interests and experiences, forms of life, and the very general facts of nature relate to the linguistic practices which are adopted.

MATHEMATICS

Some difficulties in understanding Wittgenstein's philosophy of mathematics are resolved by observing a number of integral connections with central ideas in his later work, especially the notions of grammar and rules. He held that what distinguished a mathematical symbol from a vacuous sign is that there are rules for its use within linguistic practice (*LFM*, p. 112). Recognizing that mathematical propositions are rules and applying his account of necessity to them makes comprehending the point of Wittgenstein's remarks easier. He employed his ideas about grammar and rules to argue that mathematical propositions were grammatical rules. Consideration of an example of Wittgenstein's concern with the notion of infinity provides insight into the nature of his approach. He distinguished different sorts of use of the concept and discussed the employment of infinity in the context of describing the physical world (*PR*, p. 305). Wittgenstein considered whether the notion of infinity could be applied to reality and asked how in experiential terms the meaning of a phrase about the number of a series of spheres being infinite is to be understood. Infinity is not characterized as something which has been encountered in experience but rather as a series with a beginning which continues forever. Wittgenstein commented that if the concept of an infinite number of spheres is construed along the lines of an experiment in which there could be an increasing number of spheres in a series confirming a supposition about infinity, the difference between the notions of infinite and finite is manifested.

Wittgenstein maintained that the meaning of a mathematical proposition is constituted by its proof. It must be possible to survey a proof in its entirety which means that the connections between its parts should be perspicuous. A proof gives a grammatical rule, that is, a mathematical proposition. He thought that it is misleading to think that a proof demonstrates that a mathematical proposition is true. The proof of an unprovable mathematical proposition indicates what is counted as being unprovable. It is important to distinguish between mathematical proofs which straightforwardly apply an established proof system and those which extend or change it. The former kind of proofs follow existing rules (*LFM*, p. 238 and *RFM*, p. 313). For instance, the addition of two natural numbers would follow the rules for combining them. At any point in the proof it is possible to decide not to follow the rules and to do something different (just as one can choose not to follow any other rule). A consequence of this is that the granting of certain axioms and rules of inference does not mean that the conclusion of the proof must be accepted. Not following the rules of a proof means that the proof system is no longer being applied. For example, it is possible to claim that '5 + 7 = 29' but this would not be called addition. An individual who does not acknowledge a proof or calculation within an established system has parted company with the linguistic community (*RFM*, p. 60). Obtaining a particular result from a calculation indicates that the rules in the proof have been followed correctly (*RFM*, p. 228). There is no standard of correctness over and beyond this. It might be claimed that this is an inadequate norm of correctness but the objection is effectively one to Wittgenstein's position that grammar is arbitrary. The apparent logical necessity which links axioms and rules of inference to their conclusions is actually the practice of following certain rules (*LFM*, p. 241). Mathematical proofs which extend or change an accepted proof system establish new rules to be followed. For instance, introducing addition for complex numbers (those containing the square root of -1) would extend the rules for the natural numbers. These new rules are not predetermined by the existing ones (as the application of existing proof techniques to new areas alters the rules involved) (*RFM*, pp. 268–70). What form these rules should take is not determined by logical necessity. New rule formations should be surveyable (*RFM*, pp. 150f. and 158f.) and may be subject to certain standards, such as those governing accepted forms of mathematical expressions. However, there are alternatives to the rules being proposed in any given case. For example, there were debates about the merits of extending the number system to include complex numbers.

The position that mathematical propositions are grammatical rules is from many points of view radical indeed. For instance, Wittgenstein held that epistemological questions which have traditionally been important in the philosophy of mathematics, such as those about how mathematical objects can be known, no longer have a role to play. He was opposed to the project of providing mathematics with foundations. The major approaches which Wittgenstein considered and rejected were those of logicism (see Chapter 2), intuitionism and formalism. His position differed from all these schools because he held that mathematical propositions are grammatical rules. Wittgenstein thought that mathematics did not require any foundations and that attempts to supply them were unsuccessful because what they actually created was just further mathematical propositions. This is an application of his general view that it is not possible to get behind the rules of grammar because grammar is arbitrary and that any deeper explanation would just be a further grammatical rule which stands in the same relation to linguistic usage as the rules that it supposedly explains. Wittgenstein also criticized specific aspects of the positions of logicism, intuitionism and formalism. He objected to the logicist view that the problem posed by paradoxes, such as Russell's, could be overcome by the construction of logical systems (*RFM*, pp. 120–22). These systems are just further mathematical propositions and cannot supply a deeper explanation because none is possible. The intuitionist position is that intuitions and constructions which are experienced in the mathematician's mind differ from their representation and communication in language. Intuitionism regards mathematics as being produced by the creative processes of the mathematician. Wittgenstein shared the intuitionist idea that mathematics is grounded upon human activity but was critical of a number of aspects of intuitionism. In intuitionism the truth of a mathematical proposition is connected to knowledge about that particular proposition. A proposition is true if it has been proved and false if it has been refuted (by demonstrating that the assumption that it has been proved leads to a contradiction). It follows that there are meaningful mathematical propositions which should be regarded as neither true or false (since they are undecidable in principle). In contrast, Wittgenstein argued that propositions of this kind should not be regarded as lacking a truth value but rather as meaningless (*PR*, p. 210 and *PG*, p. 458). Formalism draws upon finitist methods for proving consistency. These methods use notions that can be perceptually instantiated, namely physical signs, and make inferences from these notions to other mathematical concepts. According to formalism these methods did not raise any philosophical problems and foundational problems were to be removed by treating them in this finitistically reducible manner. Wittgenstein shared the formalist view that mathematics is about operating with signs but differed in claiming that parts of mathematics without direct application to reality must be linked to parts that have.

Wittgenstein offered an account of how the employment of mathematical propositions as norms of representation may be used to explain the nature of applied and pure mathematics. The linguistic community decides which of these propositions are to be adopted as norms of representation. Mathematical propositions are norms for forming empirical propositions and descriptions of reality which contravene them are unintelligible (*RFM*, pp. 363, 425, and 431). Arithmetic propositions are norms for describing the numbers of objects in reality and as such they operate as substitution rules (*PG*, p. 347 and *RFM*, pp. 98f.). For example, it is nonsense to assert that there are two groups of five people so there are nine people in total. In a similar fashion geometrical propositions are norms for describing spatial relations and for measurement. For instance, they are rules for the application of words such as 'length' and 'equal length' (*LFM*, p. 256). Wittgenstein's view that mathematical propositions are employed as norms of representation has some plausibility as an account of applied mathematics as it identifies how these propositions interact with discourse about reality. He argued that mathematics must have some application to reality if it is not solely to be an exercise in manipulating signs.

There is dispute over whether Wittgenstein's professed philosophical methodology is consistent with his detailed practice in the philosophy of mathematics. Although some commentators maintain that it is there seems to be a strong possibility of inconsistency between the two. For example, Wittgenstein's concerns about infinity pose this problem. One aspect of this was his exposition of the difference between infinite and finite sets (or classes) through his use of the terms 'intensional' and 'extensional'. Wittgenstein thought that there was a fundamental category difference between finite and infinite sets and methods of reasoning which are intelligible in the former domain are inappropriate in the latter situation (*PG*, pp. 460ff.). For instance, he commented that ' "infinite class" and "finite class" are different logical categories' (*PG*, p. 464). Wittgenstein claimed that the intensional and the extensional concepts of a set are grammatically different. An intensional conception of a set is defined by the satisfaction of a predicate, such as that of being a real number, and an extensional conception of a set is defined by a list of its elements, such as a list of all the prime numbers less than nine. An infinite set can only have an intensional conception (*AWL*, p. 206). If the notion of a set is introduced extensionally, then there are no such things as infinite sets. Prima facie this example does seem to be a case where Wittgenstein was leaning towards a finitist position. More technical cases from Wittgenstein's discussion of constructive mathematics raise the problem of inconsistency between his professed methodology and actual practice particularly sharply. For instance, he rejected the use of classical quantification theory in arithmetic and was interested in an alternative conception of arithmetic predicated on strongly finitist assumptions. Once again Wittgenstein's strongly finitist perspective appears to contrast with his professed methodology. So far there is no significant consensus among scholars about this question of inconsistency.

CHAPTER 7

PHILOSOPHY OF MIND

PERSPECTIVES

Wittgenstein thought that the everyday employment of psychological concepts is a source of philosophical problems. The creation of a specially constructed scientifically grounded language for psychological concepts would not resolve all the problems in the philosophy of mind because this would not address the confusion generated by the employment of ordinary psychological words. He observed that it should not come as a surprise that psychological words have complex, overlapping and not always consistent uses, because they are part of ordinary language. Psychological concepts can be and are modified. Features of the employment of psychological words are potentially misleading and it is hard to be clear about this.

Wittgenstein undertook a large-scale inquiry into the nature of ordinary psychological concepts which was limited to the description of how psychological words are employed. For example, philosophical questions about consciousness should be approached by considering the employment of the word 'consciousness'. Nothing of interest is concealed and the investigation is about what can be observed, namely, the variety of uses of psychological words. Wittgenstein thought that many problems in the philosophy of mind had their roots in a disregard for distinctions between psychological concepts. Philosophers tend not to see the complexity of usage due to their prejudices and desire to simplify the things being considered so that they can be fitted into some general or overarching account (*BB*, pp. 17f.). Obtaining a perspicuous representation of the grammatical rules governing the use of psychological words is difficult. Possible methods for creating perspicuous representations of these words should identify their similarities and divergences. Wittgenstein stressed how psychological concepts differ individually. For example, a language could be invented in which the feature of diverse usage within a single psychological word was marked by the employment of a different word for each sort of use (*BB*, p. 22). His idea was to state the features of various sorts of psychological concepts in terms of what it makes sense to say of a particular notion. The groupings for psychological words differentiated by Wittgenstein's classifications are governed by what he regarded as guidelines for being included in a particular group.

Wittgenstein held that philosophy should not proffer theories and thus he was opposed to the construction of philosophical theories about the nature of the mind. On this view major accounts, such as functionalism (which is the view that if the whole functional structure of a mind, that is including memory, dislikes, and so on, were reproduced on a system, whether biological or not, all the mental attributes of that mind would be reproduced as well), must be eschewed. Wittgenstein argued that psychological words cannot be explained or defined through the act of observing the contents of one's mind via introspection (*RPPI*, §212). This is because these words do not stand for mental phenomena. Wittgenstein applied his distinction between philosophy and science when he claimed that psychological and neuroscientific investigations into the brain were not relevant to philosophy. He thought that the creation and evaluation of empirical models of how the mind operates is the work of psychologists. Psychology investigates the causal mechanisms which link mental phenomena. to their behavioural manifestations. Wittgenstein disagreed with the idea that the difficulties of psychology arise from its being a 'young science' (*PI*, p. 232 and *RPPI*, §1039). He thought that they stemmed from conceptual problems. The origins and causes of mental phenomena and abilities which bring about various kinds of behaviour can successfully be studied by experimental psychology and neuroscientific investigation into particular brain functions. However, these experimental methods do not address philosophical difficulties (*RPPI*, §1093).

Genuine advances in psychology can result from the dissolution of its conceptual problems using philosophy. Wittgenstein held that the concepts of psychology are mostly 'just everyday concepts' (*RPPII*, §62). He would not have objected to the introduction into experimental psychology of new technical terms which replace ordinary psychological concepts by brain state ones. However, this possibility of substitution will not solve philosophical problems arising from the ordinary use of psychological concepts. Empirical theories in psychology take these concepts for granted. For example, theories of perception presume the ordinary concept of perception which is characterized by the grammatical features of words like 'seeing'. Philosophical progress consists in the clarification of what is regarded as perceiving something. This conception can then be used to test scientific theories about the relationship between certain perceptions and particular brain states.

Wittgenstein was opposed to the position that mental phenomena must be identical with brain states. In contrast, he thought that although some mental phenomena are correlated with specific brain states (*PI*, §§376 and 412) it is possible that mental phenomena are present without accompanying brain states of a specific kind. He commented that 'No supposition seems to me more natural than there is no process in the brain correlated with associating or thinking; so that it would be impossible to read off thought-processes from brain-processes' (*Z*, §608). It should be observed that Wittgenstein supported an even stronger version of this kind of rejection about the parallel existence of mental and brain phenomena. He argued that mental phenomena could be present without any accompanying brain states whatsoever. Wittgenstein remarked (*RPPI*, §1063) that 'Thinking in terms of physiological processes is extremely dangerous in connection with the clarification of conceptual problems in psychology'. It is sometimes mistakenly claimed that both the weaker and stronger versions of his view that mental phenomena exist without associated brain states commit him to the rejection of a highly successful regulative principle of the neurosciences that there must be a causal explanation of mental processes. What Wittgenstein actually maintained was the philosophical point that concepts of brain states play no role in our explanation and application of mental terms. There are no conceptual connections between brain states and mental phenomena. A related point is that even if it could be established that mental phenomena are invariably accompanied by brain states of a specific kind it would not follow that statements about mental phenomena must be descriptions of brain states. (For example, first person present tense psychological sentences are generally not descriptions of any kind.)

Wittgenstein disagreed with the view that ordinary psychological concepts belong to an elementary (scientific) theory which causally explains behaviour. These concepts are not part of any theory for explaining or predicting behaviour. This idea that ordinary psychological concepts belong to an elementary behavioural theory supports the view that progress in experimental psychology and neuroscience can and should lead to the replacement of this elementary theory by a more advanced scientifically grounded one. Wittgenstein would have thought that replacing ordinary psychological concepts with brain state ones would have the consequence that it would no longer be possible to adequately account for human action. He held that scientific causal explanations could not make human action intelligible. This view is a specific case of Wittgenstein's general rejection of causal theories of intentionality. He thought that psychological concepts were employed to explain behaviour in a teleological and not a causal fashion. If behaviour was necessitated by causes it would cease to be intentional. He claimed that unlike brain state concepts psychological ones do not have the primary or even the exclusive function of explaining, predicting and controlling behaviour. The roles of such concepts are as diverse as human life (*RPPII*, §35) itself and brain state concepts could not take any of their places satisfactorily.

Wittgenstein used the contrast between inner and outer to characterize the picture that a person can directly observe the contents of his mind through introspection, whilst others can only ever witness his mental states via the consequences they have on his body and behaviour. This picture informs many positions in the philosophy of mind including some that do not appear to fit it at first sight. Materialism adhered to this picture but maintained that the mind has to be material so the traditional dualism of mind and body becomes that of brain and body. Here the brain is cast in the role of the inner. Wittgenstein challenged materialism in a variety of ways. For example, he insisted that psychological terms could only be applied to living beings, especially humans. He remarked that 'Only of a living human being and what resembles (behaves like) a living human being can one say that it has sensations; it sees, is blind; hears; is deaf; is conscious or unconscious' (*PI*, §281). On this view they could not solely be applied to the brain and so the materialist position is undermined. A commonly discussed issue about Wittgenstein's philosophy of mind is whether he was actually a behaviourist. For example, unlike behaviourism he did not claim that one infers propositions from descriptions of mere bodily movement but argued instead that behaviour is described from the start in mental terms. This is a complex issue but there is widespread consensus that if he was a behaviourist at all then it was not in a simple and straightforward fashion.

CLASSIFYING MENTAL CONCEPTS

The scale and complexity of Wittgenstein's classification of psychological concepts precludes anything other than a very selective treatment of some its aspects. It is hoped that the reader will gain some insight into how to recognize Wittgenstein's classificatory remarks as such and thus be better able to make effective use of more detailed treatments, such as Budd (1989), of these matters. Wittgenstein envisaged the formation of a genealogical tree of psychological concepts which would show their systematic typology. This tree which while not necessarily precise would be a perspicuous representation (*RPPI*, §895). He sought to represent a logical order which displays the relations among psychological concepts (*RPPI*, §722). The first attempt (*RPPI*, §836) at this typology was less promising than the second (*RPPII*, §§63 and 148). In the latter he divided psychological concepts into those of sensations, images and emotions. Sensations have genuine duration, are capable of simultaneous occurrence, admit of degrees and qualitative mixtures, inform us about the material world and have bodily location. Images do not inform us about the material world and are subject to the will. Emotions are characterized by genuine duration, typical feelings (which colour thoughts) and mimetic expression, and a lack of bodily location. They are divided into directed emotional dispositions (like loving), undirected emotional dispositions (like depression), undirected occurrent emotions (like worry) and directed occurrent emotions (like becoming angry at an event). Many of the distinctions he drew in these two typologies are retained and elaborated in great detail in subsequent remarks but not in order to contribute to systematic typology. Wittgenstein made no further attempts to construct a systematic typology and there is some evidence that he came to think such efforts were futile. Indeed, there is no reason to suppose that there is a fruitful system of classification which will locate each psychological concept in its appropriate place in the order. This is because psychological concepts did not come into being as classificatory concepts for mental phenomena.

Wittgenstein sought to distinguish psychological concepts from one another individually. His idea was to state the features of various sorts of psychological concepts in terms of what it makes sense to say of a particular notion. It is possible to identify different kinds of employment found within the use of a single psychological word and make broad classifications between sorts of psychological words. For example, different sorts of usage can be located within a single psychological verb since words such as 'believe', 'expect' and 'fear' are used in diverse ways (*BB*, pp. 19–22). One classification that Wittgenstein used was into mental acts (such as mental calculation), events (such as hearing a noise), processes (such as having images) and states (such as occurrent emotions). Each of these groups has particular individual characteristics. For instance, it is possible to perform an activity more or less successfully as one can calculate well or badly. He emphasized that this classification should not be regarded as a rigid foundation for analysis in the philosophy of mind as forcing psychological concepts into particular classificatory groups (regardless of attention to individual differences) distorts them (*RPPI*, §648). The notion of genuine duration is important for the classification of psychological words. Wittgenstein characterized the notion of genuine duration in terms of a group of related concepts. One of these is that it must be possible to specify the beginning and end (between which there is continuous persistence) of a psychological phenomenon that is described by the notion (*Z*, §472). Another feature is that it can be spot checked (*RPPI*, §51). For example, it makes sense to ask at any instant whether a sensation, such as pain, is still going on whilst this question does not make sense with regard to belief. Genuine duration may be interrupted by breaks in consciousness or attention (*RPPII*, §45) and it has a uniform or non-uniform course over time (*Z*, §488). For example, Wittgenstein used the notion of genuine duration to distinguish between sensations, felt emotions, moods, thinking, concentrating and felt desires from believing, understanding, meaning or intending.

Intentional attitudes including believing, intending and meaning something do not signify mental activities, events, processes or states (*Z*, §§78–85, *PI*, p. 59n, *RPPI*, §836, *RPPII*, §§45–50 and 63). These attitudes are not activities since they cannot be performed more or less successfully. For example, one cannot more or less successfully mean something (*PI*, §§674–81). Another reason for not being activities is that intentional attitudes are mostly not subject to the will. For instance, one cannot decide to intend something (*Z*, §§46f.). Intentional attitudes are not involuntary events or processes because they cannot have temporal duration, or be slowed down, reversed or left unfinished. For example, a belief that something is the case could not be left unfinished. Intentional attitudes are not states because they lack genuine duration (*Z*, §45 and *RPPII* §45). A state is something which can be interrupted whereas an intentional attitude cannot. Also at any time one can intend indefinitely many things but not be in indefinitely many different mental states. Wittgenstein argued that the tendency to regard accounts which explain sensation as a paradigm to which all other explanations of mental processes or states should be assimilated involves disregarding important grammatical distinctions (*Z*, §§490 and 507). He remarked that 'love is not a feeling. Love is put to the test, pain not. One does not say: "That was not true pain, or it would not have gone off so quickly" ' (*Z*, §504).

Another aspect of Wittgenstein's philosophy of mind was his treatment of the concept of pretence. He considered different kinds of pretence, such as pretending to read (*PI*, §156) and to be in pain (*PI*, §250). His general views can usefully be illustrated by examining the instance of pain. Wittgenstein thought that pretence about being in pain (which is a special case of the absence of pain in the presence of pain behaviour) utilizes the usual background to pain, such as pain typically manifesting itself in pain behaviour (*PI*, pp. 228f., *Z*, §571 and *LWII*, p. 86). This is evident if the case of pretending to be in pain in different circumstances is examined. Depending on the circumstances there will be different views about whether someone is pretending or not. It is not always legitimate to doubt that there is pain when there is pain behaviour. Sometimes there is no doubt that a person is not pretending. Wittgenstein remarked that ' "But, if you are *certain*, isn't it that you are shutting your eyes in face of doubt?" – They are shut' (*PI*, p. 224). Sometimes it is clear that someone is pretending. Lastly, sometimes it is hard to be sure whether the person is pretending or not. What the example shows is that depending on the circumstances there may be a problem about deciding or agreeing in judgement whether there is pretence about being in pain.

The difference between first and third person present tense psychological sentences plays a very significant role in Wittgenstein's classification and analysis of mental concepts. The apparent similarity in grammar between sentences, such as 'I am in pain' and 'he is in pain', contribute to a misleading picture of the mind. He argued that it is an error to explain the distinction between first and third person present tense psychological sentences by the idea that an individual can directly observe the contents of his mind through introspection, whilst others can only ever witness his mental phenomena through bodily and behavioural manifestations. Wittgenstein criticized the associated claim that since knowledge about one's sensations is derived from introspection this cannot be mistaken and rejected its corollary that as knowledge of others' sensations cannot be acquired through introspection it can never be as certain as knowledge about one's self. Wittgenstein commented that 'It is correct to say "I know what you are thinking", and wrong to say "I know what I am thinking. (A whole cloud of philosophy condensed into a drop of grammar)"' (*PI*, p. 222). He offered an expressive account of first person present tense psychological sentences, such as 'I am in pain'. He claimed that such sentences are not descriptions of any sort and have no evidential grounds for their assertion (*PI*, §246). He would have repudiated the view shared by dualism and materialism that these sentences describe psychological or brain phenomena. Wittgenstein claimed that first person present tense psychological sentences are akin to natural non-linguistic expressions of mental states, such as smiling (*PI*, §244 and *RPPI*, §305). He thought that third person present tense psychological sentences, such as 'Jones is in pain', are asserted or verified upon behavioural grounds (*PI*, §303).

Wittgenstein's philosophy of mind repeatedly returned to aspect seeing from 1935 onwards and it was a very significant theme in his writings from 1947–9. It importantly featured in part two of the *Investigations*, and in both volumes of *Remarks on the Philosophy of Psychology* and the *Last Writings*. The differences between the grammar of aspect seeing and that of various kinds of seeing provided insight into the character of the former. Wittgenstein began the treatment of aspect seeing in part two of the *Investigations* by considering some uses of the word 'see'. He remarked about two employments of the term 'see' that (*PI*, p. 193):

The one: 'What do you see there?' – 'I see this' (and then a description, a drawing, a copy). The other: 'I see a likeness between these two faces' – let the man I tell this to be seeing the faces as clearly as I do myself. /The importance of this is the difference of category between the two 'objects' of sight.

Wittgenstein also commented that 'The expression of a change of aspect is the expression of a *new* perception and at the same time of the perception's being unchanged' (*PI*, p. 196) and that aspect seeing was not part of perception which meant that it was both like and unlike seeing (*PI*, p. 197). What these remarks indicate is that Wittgenstein thought that aspect seeing denoted a collection of connected perceptual concepts. A change of aspect occurs when certain objects, especially pictorial ones, can be viewed as having more than one aspect. For example, an individual could look at a figure of a duck-rabbit (*PI*, p. 194) and not see a duck in it. Similarly a person might look at a double cross figure (*PI*, p. 207) but not see that there is a white cross in addition to the black cross. Aspect change occurs when a previously unnoticed facet of an object becomes apparent and is thus seen as something different. For instance, in the case of the duck-rabbit aspect change would have occurred if an individual had moved from perceiving it as a picture of a rabbit to that of a duck. Another case would be that an individual had experienced an aspect change if whilst looking at an object he said 'Now it is . . .' or talked as if he '*saw* a different object every time' *RPPII*, §642. Simply reproducing or describing an object in an alternative way would not in itself indicate that a change of aspect had taken place. The puzzle which Wittgenstein sought to resolve was that of how it could be that an object is seen differently although the object has not changed. Upon first inspection it both appears to have altered and not altered (*LWI*, §§493f.). For Wittgenstein this seeming paradox about change raised the issue of whether aspect seeing should be regarded as an instance of seeing or thinking. The treatment of this matter dominated his discussion of the topic but ultimately he thought that aspect seeing had affinities with both seeing which is a state (*PI*, p. 203, *RPPI*, §8 and *RPPII*, §388) and thinking which is an action (*PI*, p. 212, *RPPII*, §544 and *LWI*, §451). Wittgenstein claimed that kinds of aspect seeing differed according to the extent of thought involved in them (*PI*, p. 207, *LWI*, §582 and *RPPI*, §970). The apparent paradox of aspect seeing was at least in part generated by the fact that what was seen in the usual sense had not altered but what was seen in the sense of being allied to thinking had. Aspect change was not an alteration of perception but of attitude.

PRIVATE LANGUAGE

One of the few claims about the private language argument[1] which (nearly) all commentators would be in accord about is that, to say the least, it is not straightforward. Different philosophers take Wittgenstein's remarks about private language in diverse incongruous ways and there are a wide variety of substantially dissimilar interpretations about what it is that is actually being argued. Arguably Wittgenstein's views about rule-following were an essential part of the conceptual framework of the private language argument. The key notions of rule-following for present purposes are those pertaining to the distinction between being in accord with a rule and following a rule. Wittgenstein's conception of following a rule is notable because it is central to the question of whether it is possible to follow a rule privately. It is essential to inspect his handling of this issue due to the role that it plays in the private language argument. It is important that the idea of private rules is not misunderstood here. The following two senses of privacy are unproblematic. An individual can follow a rule which is particular to that speaker and also rules which are not known to any other members of the linguistic community. Wittgenstein thought that private rules cannot be followed if they are taken to be rules which are in principle incomprehensible to anyone else apart from the speaker. It is impossible for these rules to have an expression in public language. The problem with private rule-following is related to the objectivity of according with a rule. Whether a person is conforming to a rule in practice is not set by whether the person thinks that he is conforming. Rather, it is determined by that which is considered as conforming to a norm of regularity in practice. (This norm of regularity is related to behaviour which is public.) In order for a rule to be really followed there has to be a norm of regularity in practice. Therefore it is impossible to follow rules in private as there is no technique of conforming with a rule and a person's comprehension of the rule would not be shown in practice.

It is useful to briefly outline what Wittgenstein took a private language to be as there is sometimes confusion about this when considering cases of what is and is not a private language. He defined a private language with respect to two properties and a consequence which is derived from them (*PI*, §243). The first feature is that the words of the private language are to refer to what can only be known to the person who is speaking. The second is that the words of this language are to refer to the immediate private sensations of the person speaking. These attributes are elucidated further as the private language argument is developed. Taking both these aspects, Wittgenstein concluded that another person cannot understand the private language. It should be noted that this latter claim is not giving a fundamental characteristic of a private language. That is, a language which is incomprehensible to anyone but the speaker or peculiar to an individual speaker does not have to be a private one. It will become evident that this enabled Wittgenstein to distinguish between the trivial and important traits of the concept of privacy. His aim in the private language argument was to demonstrate that a language of this kind is not possible.

A significant rendering of the private language argument regards it as being directed against the Cartesian conception[2] of the mind.[3] The reading of the private language argument as being directed against the Cartesian conception of the mind is not wholly without its difficulties. Wittgenstein provided no textual indication at all about precisely what the intended target of the argument was. For present purposes, there are two ways of handling this lacuna concerning textual evidence. One is to attempt to deduce what the objective of the argument was and the other is to take the view that it is not intended to have an exact target. Given that there is no direct textual evidence, factors about the place which the private language argument has within his philosophies of language and mind come into play. The key ground which supports the idea that the focus of the argument is opposition to the Cartesian conception of the mind concerns the scope of this notion. For example, the main reason which Hacker (1986, pp. 255ff.) gives is that the Cartesian conception of the mind covers a considerable diversity of different positions. However, this ground is not entirely convincing in itself. This is because there is the question of why Wittgenstein would have elected to direct the private language argument against this particular conception if it was possible not to specify a precise target and thus retain the option of the argument as having a wider critical sweep. (Of course, this claim presupposes the view that everything being equal it is preferable to regard the argument as being more extensively applicable.) It is now appropriate to investigate the second alternative with respect to the lack of textual discussion, namely, that the private language argument is not intended to have a strict target. A version of this sort of rendering of the argument will be presented here. In general terms, the presentation offered is that the private language argument is aimed at opposing the concept of a private object. From this perspective the deficiencies of the Cartesian conception of the mind can be viewed as being a case which comes under the remit of this critique of the notion of a private object. The characterization of an idea of a private object is just that it is any private object at all regardless of its nature. The precise nature of the private object, such as whether it is a private sensation or a private emotion, is not crucial here. However, the important feature of a private object is that it is an object which is employed in private rule-following. That is, a rule is followed privately in the sense that accord with a rule is decided by comparison with a private object. Given the favoured presentation of the private language argument it is possible to formulate it in different ways depending upon the position which is being criticized. For example, the number of critiques that there are in the argument against the idea of private sensation is contingent upon the variants of the accounts of the concept of private sensation which are being offered. Some grounds for the plausibility of the preferred presentation of the private language argument are those of how the argument can be expressed using the notion of a private object.

The basic perspective of the favoured presentation of the private language argument has been given and it is appropriate to look at the lines of argument in more detail. The argument can be presented with a private object taking the place of the more specific instances of private objects, such as private pain in §253, which are found in the *Investigations*.[4] As has been noted, Wittgenstein supplied a preliminary definition of a private language with respect to two properties and an implication which follows from them (§243). He then considered the idea of reference to mental states (§§244f.). Wittgenstein remarked that the linguistic employment of a word is not a private language when it is frequently possible for others to know when a person is in the state which the word refers to. He suggested that in answer to the question of how do words refer to states that the word for a state is learnt in conjunction with the natural expression of a state. The verbal manifestation of a state is itself an articulation of a state (§244). The two properties which constitute Wittgenstein's initial definition of a private language require more clarification to be entirely lucid. (They will be dealt with in the order in which they occur in §243.) The major part of the private language argument from §§246–252 is comprised of a sharpening of the idea that the words of the private language are to refer to what can only be known to the person who is speaking. The privacy of the objects is the extent to which it is possible only for the speaker of the private language to know what they are and where they are located. The overall thrust of Wittgenstein's argument in §§246–252 was that a private object is not private when this is taken as claiming that the words of the private language are to refer to what can only be known to the person who is speaking. The assertion that private objects are private when this is interpreted as meaning that the words of the private language are to refer to what can only be known to the speaker is composed of the union of two claims which can be distinguished (§246). The first of these claims is that the speaker can know that he is in a state of mind. The second is that others can only surmise that the speaker is in that specific state. (At this juncture, it is useful to characterize the idea of privileged access and reflect on it very briefly. The idea of privileged access is the particular relationship that one has to the contents of one's own mind but that no person has to anyone else's.[5] The epistemological problem of privileged access is that of how knowledge of the mental lives of other people is possible. It is evident that the conjunction of the two differentiable claims from §246 noted above is an expression of the notion of privileged access.) Each of these two distinguishable claims was repudiated in turn by Wittgenstein. He denied that the speaker can know when he is in a state. Wittgenstein remarked that it is not possible to say of the speaker at all that he can know that he is in a state. Neither is it possible to maintain that others are unable to learn that the speaker is in a state from his behaviour since this suggests that the speaker learns of his state. However, it is not possible to assert that the speaker learns of his state because he has the state (§246). The claim that the speaker can know when he is in a state has two possible construals, namely, that this is a statement about an empirical matter or about a grammatical one. The claim is not an empirical statement but the form of the statement encourages misconstrual of this kind (and thereby promotes the mistaken position that since it is not possible for the speaker to doubt his states he must know of them) (§251). If the claim is taken to be a statement about grammar then it is saying that it does not make sense to assert that the speaker doubts whether he is in a state. The idea that there could be doubt about the state is ruled out. What it is not is a description of part of a speaker's mental states. Wittgenstein commented that this is how the claim should be understood. The concept of privileged access sheds useful illumination on what is occurring here. There appears to be privileged access but what is actually happening is that the utterance of doubt is ruled out in the case of the person who is speaking about his state (§247). Wittgenstein also rejected the second claim, namely, the view that others can only surmise that the speaker is in a state (§246). There are two ways of taking this assertion. In a sense, the claim is incorrect in that if the word 'know' is regarded as having its usual employment because it is frequently possible for others to know when the speaker is in a state. (Wittgenstein noted that sometimes a person is transparent to others. However, it is also possible for a person to be wholly enigmatic to another. For instance, this may become apparent when a person is in a country with a radically different culture (p. 223).) If the claim is understood in another fashion then it is nonsense. This is because if the word 'know' is deemed to mean knowledge in such a manner that doubt is logically ruled out then the claim does not make sense as it is only possible to have knowledge where there could be doubt. (It is worth noticing at this point that a ground for holding the view that it is impossible for a person to know if another individual is in a state is that there could always be pretence. In response to this view Wittgenstein thought that it does not invariably make sense to assume that there is pretence occurring, such as with children (p. 229).) A general conclusion to be drawn from the argument above about the concept of privacy is that the idea of privileged access is misguided. A private object is private when this is taken as claiming that it is not exhibited and it ceases to be private if it is disclosed (p. 222). This sense of privacy is clearly not that propounded by the concept of privileged access.

The second key property of Wittgenstein's initial definition of a private language needs examination. The preponderance of the private language argument from §§253–255 consists of an elucidation of the notion that the words of the private language are to refer to the immediate private objects of the person who is speaking. The private objects belong to the speaker and it is not possible for them to belong to another person. (This characterizes the idea of privacy of ownership.) Wittgenstein's argument in §§253–255 was generally focused upon the idea that a private object is not private when this is understood as maintaining that the words of the private language are to refer to the immediate private objects of the speaker. The claim that private objects are private when this is taken to mean that the words of the private language are to refer to immediate private objects of the person who is speaking is stating that other people cannot have the speaker's immediate private objects (or alternatively put only the speaker can have his immediate private objects) (§253). The position that it is solely the person who is speaking who can have his immediate private objects raises two issues which need examination. The first of these topics is what does it mean to talk about the idea of having here. (A more precise formulation of this question is what determines the owner of a private object.) The second matter is that supposing the position that if the immediate private objects are the speaker's he must have them, is it possible for others to have them in addition to the speaker? Before proceeding further with the issues about the ownership of immediate private objects it is opportune to reflect upon the interpretation of the concept of criteria (as the term plays a role in the argument of §253).

It is appropriate to take up the matter of Wittgenstein's treatment of the topics about the ownership of immediate private objects once again. His handling of the first question about what determines the owner of a private object was in terms of what was expressed. Wittgenstein commented that a private object is owned by the speaker who exhibits it (§302). The second issue, which is that supposing the position that if the immediate private objects are the speaker's he must have them is it possible for others to have them in addition to the speaker, involves the notion of a criterion in its presentation (§253). The difficulty is what is a criterion for the identity of private objects. The assertion that it is only possible for the speaker to have his private objects is a statement about grammar which is akin to the claim that if the private objects are the speaker's private objects then he has them. A different kind of problem with the assertion is that the view that it is only possible for the speaker to have his X applies to a considerable number of entities which are publicly observable in addition to private objects. Taken in this way it is possible to accept the position that private objects have a special privacy of ownership but what this claim does not demonstrate is that private objects are private in a sense which does not apply to publicly observable entities. It is nonsense to maintain that a particular private object is the speaker's unless this statement is construed as meaning that there is no such thing as having a private object and questioning who the private object belongs to. When considering the identity of private objects it is crucial to resist the temptation to see the issues as though they were metaphysical impossibilities. The position that other people cannot have the speaker's immediate private objects is the articulation of a rule of grammar that bars statements of the form that one person had another's private object from linguistic employment. For instance, the sentence 'I have your toothache' is nonsense. The appearance that the words of the private language are to refer to the immediate private objects of the person who is speaking is actually a ruling out of statements of this sort. An overall consequence which arises out of the above argument concerning the idea of privacy is the same as that which emerges from the discussion of the first key property of a private language. This is that a private object is private when this is taken as claiming that it is not expressed and it ceases to be private if it is communicated.

The private language argument proceeds by preparing the argumentative ground which leads up to the consideration of the idea of attaching a linguistic expression to a private object. Wittgenstein remarked that if words refer to states in the sense that the word for a state is learnt in conjunction with the natural expression of a state then the word is not part of a private language (§256). He augmented this point by claiming that nothing is achieved by postulating the supposition that there is a state which has no natural expression as the linguistic articulation of states of this kind is not part of the normal practice of the community of language users (§257). A reason for this is that the usual linguistic practice concerning states assumes that there are publicly observable manifestations of a state. Having dismissed the acceptability of the presupposition that there is a state that has no natural expression, Wittgenstein discussed the idea of a state which differs from the linguistic community's ordinary conception of a state only in the respect that it can only be known to the person who is speaking (that is, it is a privileged access state) (§258). A linguistic association (a sign) is attached to this privileged access state. Wittgenstein claimed that the sign has to be part of a private language. He held that the sign must be characterized for the speaker only and the meaning of a sign is the privileged access state that it is correlated with by virtue of a private ostensive definition. The private ostensive definition is by attending to the privileged access state and connecting a sign to the state. Wittgenstein thought that it was not possible to create a link between a sign and the privileged access state of a suitable sort. To understand this point it is necessary to consider the relationship between private ostensive definitions and private rule-following. A private ostensive definition is a private rule justifying the employment of a sign. In these cases of private rule-following there is no technique of conforming with a rule because exhibiting a private experience (in the way in which the private linguist understands privacy) is not possible. Thus these instances of rule-following in private are ones in which it is possible only for the speaker to know whether they are being followed and thus they are basically privileged access rules. It is impossible to differentiate between the correct employment of a private rule from the usage which appears to be correct to the speaker. The above argument indicates why there is no connection of the required kind between a sign and the privileged access state (§258).

Having given the favoured presentation of the private language argument, it is useful to briefly consider two general issues about the argument. The first of these is how compatible is realism with the idea that the correct usage of a private rule cannot be distinguished from the employment which seems to be correct to the speaker. From a realist point of view there is a difference between the correct application of a private rule and the usage which appears to be right to the person who is speaking even if it is not known what this difference is. Given this perspective, the lack of a technique for conforming with a rule because it is followed in private does not affect the difference about correctness in rule-following. It should be noted that the realist standpoint here is in opposition to Wittgenstein's position that in order for a rule to be really followed there has to be a norm of regularity in practice. What these remarks above suggest is that there may be some difficulty in adhering to both a realist point of view and the favoured interpretation of the private language argument. The second general topic is whether ideas about verification have a role in the private language argument. The favoured presentation of the private language argument does not rely upon verificationist premises. An example of the lack of dependence upon verificationist premises is an aspect of the view that there is no link of the required kind between a sign and the privileged access state (§258). Wittgenstein remarked on the idea of remembering the connection correctly in the future. A treatment of this which leads towards the use of a verificationist premise is to take him as positing scepticism about remembering in the sense of how it is possible for the speaker to be certain that he remembered correctly when he next designates the privileged access state. If this is handled in a verificationist way the question about remembering is essentially that of how it is possible for the speaker to find out that the remembering was correct. However, if it is dealt with in a non-verificationist manner the question then becomes one of what possible difference would remembering rightly actually make.

The ramifications of the private language argument are numerous. If the argument is interpreted as being directed against the Cartesian conception of the mind it thereby has a bearing upon both questions in epistemology and the philosophy of mind. It matters philosophically because of the indirect width of the positions which it has pertinence to. The Cartesian conception of the mind holds the grounds of language as being in the private experiences of the speaker. This perspective assumes that mental phenomena are dominant in the usage of language. It appears that all that is required for language is that words can be assigned a meaning purely within the speaker's mental life. Very roughly put, this picture of language is that the meaning of a word is the object that it is correlated with by virtue of a private ostensive definition (or alternatively expressed, by becoming familiar privately with that which the word stands for and attaching it to the word). Words acquire their meanings from what is immediately experienced by the speaker. They are meaningful to any person who has both attended to the relevant private experiences and connected these words to these experiences. It is clear that this is a fundamentally private activity. In different guises, this portrait of language permeates a number of perspectives which are powerfully established in philosophical thought. It is prominent in both the Cartesian (or rationalist) and empiricist traditions. For example, versions of it are present in Descartes and Hume. The appeal of this view of language has continued into modern philosophy with it being a characteristic trait in a good deal of the writings of the Vienna Circle. The manner in which the Cartesian conception of the mind takes the grounds of language as being in the private experiences of the speaker helps to show how the private language argument affects weighty topics in epistemology. The principal viewpoint from which a substantial range of epistemological issues are approached is one which presupposes that the basis of language is located in concentration upon the speaker's sense impressions and linking words to these impressions. This can be illustrated by considering a few epistemological ideas from some seventeenth-century empiricist philosophers. (For current purposes the differences in detail are not important.) It was assumed that a speaker's sense impressions (at minimum to the speaker himself) can be linguistically stated. There is no presumption that the speaker must have knowledge of anything except the contents of his own mind for these linguistic statements to be possible. (It is not necessary at this point to make any kind of judgement about whether there is actually anything at all outside the mind of the speaker.) Clearly espousal of this view commits one to the position that it is possible to have a private language. (This is because this view is an instance of the general idea that words acquire their meaning from the speaker's concern with the appropriate private experiences and the linkage of these words to these experiences.) Once the speaker is able to linguistically state his sense impressions and thus describe his mental phenomena, he is able to express how the world is. The epistemological force lies in the commitment that all that can be known with certainty are the contents of one's own sense impressions and secure knowledge about the world must be grounded on that of our own mental lives. Evidently, if private languages are not possible then this kind of empiricist epistemology must be abandoned as being fundamentally flawed. The general philosophical import of the private language argument is further strengthened due to its noteworthy consequences for issues in the philosophy of mind. The Cartesian conception of the mind, which deems the grounds of language as being in the private experiences of the speaker, is a supposition which underlies what might be thought of as the Cartesian account of mental phenomena. The key idea is that what is inside one in some way mirrors what is outside. That is, as entities in the world can be examined by observation it is possible, in a similar fashion, to investigate the entities which are within our own minds. The meaning of a mental term is the object, which is apprehended by introspection, that it is associated with by virtue of a private ostensive definition. (Much of Wittgenstein's general philosophy of mind was an attempt to undermine this appealing idea of how discourse about the mind operates.) This sort of Cartesian account is also present in tacit ways in modern ideas about the philosophy of mind. For example, consider the functionalist position that if the whole functional structure of a mind, that is including memory, dislikes, and so on, were reproduced on a system (whether biological or not) all the mental attributes of that mind would be reproduced as well. An assumption is that there are mental entities which can be inspected by attending to the relevant phenomena of the mind and thereby be suitably mapped. Another case arises out of the development of increasingly sophisticated models of artificial consciousness in computers. The claim that it is possible to simulate the property of consciousness is partly reliant upon the notion that the pertinent mental features for this can be discerned by observation of the mind.

CHAPTER 8

EPISTEMOLOGY, RELIGION AND AESTHETICS

EPISTEMOLOGY

On Certainty was Wittgenstein's most elaborate and significant investigation into questions about knowledge. For four separate periods during his final year and a half he was concerned with certainty and associated topics with the final entry in his notes made just two days prior to his death. In terms of its fundamental outlook Wittgenstein's attitude to epistemology in *On Certainty* greatly varied from much traditional epistemology. He did not attempt to argue against scepticism directly but rather challenged presuppositions common to both the formulation of sceptical doubts and attempts to ground knowledge. Wittgenstein took a keen and lasting interest in G.E. Moore's articles 'A Defence of Common Sense' (1925), 'Proof of the External World' (1939) and 'Certainty' (1941). The notes that comprise *On Certainty* were mostly stimulated by these papers and are concerned with a number of the same topics addressed in Moore's articles. In 'A Defence of Common Sense' Moore stated many propositions belonging to what he termed the common-sense view of reality. These are propositions which he claimed to know with certainty to be true, but which could not be justified. Propositions belonging to the common-sense view of reality are those which are held by all mankind. Moore claimed these propositions included ones such as (1959b, p. 33):

There exists at present a living human body, which is *my* body. . . . Ever since it was born, it has been either in contact with or not far from the surface of the earth; and at every moment since it was born, there have also existed many things, having shape and size in three dimensions.

For instance, no one would deny the existence of their own body unless they were engaged in philosophical activity or had what would be regarded as very odd ideas. In 'Proof of the External World' Moore maintained that a proof of the external world is required. He argued that this could be proved and known to be certain by invoking the proposition that he has two hands. This proposition can be known with certainty since it is possible to hold up one hand and then the other. However, Moore conceded that he could not prove that he has two hands because he is unable to prove that he is not dreaming. The central point of his papers was that there is a mind independent reality which is known to exist and no reasons for scepticism could be sufficient to undermine this common-sense knowledge. Knowledge does not have to be proved to be certain.

Wittgenstein wrote in response to Moore's attack on scepticism about the external world and criticized him. He agreed with Moore's view articulated in 'A Defence of Common Sense' that there is a core of common-sense propositions that are certain and therefore impervious to doubt (*OC*, §§155 and 674) but rejected the latter's account of why this is the case. Wittgenstein denied that Moore knew such propositions and repudiated his position that 'I know' is being used correctly by a philosopher who says things along the lines of 'I know there is an external world'. He thought that Moore's assertion of this or claims of a similar ilk misused the expression 'I know' as it is employed correctly only in cases where it is possible to supply evidence for or against the claim in question (*OC*, §§10, 372 and 576). However, one cannot produce evidence for or against those core common-sense propositions regarded as certain by both of them. Given Wittgenstein's view that certainty implies the absence of doubt it follows that doubt about these propositions is not really doubt at all. He maintained that knowledge of such core common-sense propositions is not something that is proved and is actually the background against which we come to acquire other knowledge (*OC*, §§288, 397 and 552). Wittgenstein attempted to distinguish between the rules of grammar for the concepts of knowing and certainty (*OC*, §8). He thought that it was correct to assert 'I am certain there is an external world' or something in a similar vein because certain can be employed in contexts where giving evidence or doubting are inappropriate (*OC*, §§193f.). It is possible that Moore's propensity to conflate certainty and knowledge is attributable to his position that both are mental states which are accessible via intro-spection (*OC*, §§13, 90 and 356). Wittgenstein objected to Moore's view on the grounds that the claim that knowing or being certain that something is a state of mind is a commitment to the position about a state of the mind (or brain) will explain the manifestations of that knowledge. He argued that neither knowledge nor certainty is a mental state which is obscured from view behind its expressions. Wittgenstein rejected Moore's view that assertions of the kind 'This is a hand' or claims of a similar ilk expressed propositions which have sense. These propositions do not have sense but they are not non-sense. Wittgenstein regarded the conclusion of Moore's proof which is that 'I know there is an external world' as senseless because knowl-edge of the proposition is not proved nor is doubt about it disproved (*OC*, §§6 and 209).

Wittgenstein supplied a picture of the nature of knowledge in *On Certainty*. He elucidated the grounds for Moore's and his view that there is a core of common-sense propositions which are certain. In *Moore and Wittgenstein on Certainty* Avrum Stroll argues that Wittgenstein provided two logically distinct accounts of the ground of certainty, namely, relative foundationalism and absolute found-ationalism. The former will be considered first. An important idea is that knowledge consists in two broad classes of propositions, namely a core of propositions that form the basis of inquiry and which are surrounded by empirical propositions that are the consequences of investigation. These core propositions constitute our world picture (*OC*, §94). Wittgenstein stressed that world picture propositions differ in kind from empirical propositions. Although they take the form of empirical propositions world picture propositions do not function as empirically testable propositions. Wittgenstein remarked that 'the *questions* that we raise and our *doubts* depend on the fact that some propositions are exempt from doubt, are as it were like hinges on which those turn' (*OC*, §341). Indeed the very language 'game of doubting itself presupposes certainty' (*OC*, §115). Wittgenstein sometimes referred to world picture type propositions as 'rules of testing', 'grammatical rules', 'scaffolding for our thoughts', and the like. One metaphor he favoured for certainty was 'standing fast'. A world picture 'is the inherited background against which I distinguish between true and false' (*OC*, §94). The world picture itself cannot be doubted. It is the background against which we come to acquire other knowledge and it provides the context in which knowledge claims are meaningful. Wittgenstein stated that it is a mistake to think that world picture propositions are explicitly learnt (*OC*, §279) but thought that we can subsequently discover which propositions these are (*OC*, §152). Wittgenstein thought that Moore's common-sense propositions were world picture propositions. People may be struck strongly by a world picture which is not theirs because of its unfamiliarity. Examples of these include world pictures held in the distant past and in radically different cultures. There can be alteration in a world picture. Wittgenstein remarked (*OC*, §92): 'Men have believed that they could make rain; why should not a king be brought up in the belief that the world began with him?' The king would believe that his birth coincided with the origin of the world because Moore's view that the world had existed before his birth would not be part of his world picture. Wittgenstein considered whether Moore could convert the king to his view and argued that if he did he would succeed by making the king see the world in a different way. One world picture may be replaced by another. Whenever world pictures change there are either gains or losses, because different world pictures are closer and less close to the truth (*OC*, §§608–612).

A world picture is a system of propositions which support one another. He remarked (*OC*, §141): 'When we first begin to *believe* anything, what we believe is not a single proposition, it is a whole system of propositions'. What is held certain is not one proposition but a system of propositions (*OC*, §225). Gradually a system of propositions is learnt, some of which are certain and indubitable whilst others are more or less open to doubt. Certain propositions do not have this status because they are intrinsically obvious or especially convincing. What propositions are certain are so by virtue of those that shift around them (*OC*, §144). Wittgenstein was aware that the propositions adopted and whether or not a particular proposition was plausible depended upon the world picture. A proposition is implausible in a particular world picture and may cease to be so if this alters or is replaced by another (*OC*, §§161f.). Wittgenstein's position that a world picture is a system of propositions diverges from Moore's view that common-sense propositions do not form a system. It also differs from that of Descartes who regarded the *cogito* as the sole foundation of knowledge. The world picture provides the framework for inquiry. Questions cannot be asked about the world picture itself but within a particular world picture they can be posed. World picture propositions function as rules of testing but are not tested themselves. Wittgenstein commented (*OC*, §105):

> All testing, all confirmation and all disconfirmation of a hypothesis takes place already within a system. And this system is not a more or less arbitrary and doubtful point of departure for all our arguments: no, it belongs to the essence of what we call an argument. The system is not so much the point of departure, as the element in which arguments have their life.

Almost every proposition can be revised but the probability of each proposition being revised is not the same. Revising certain propositions might be avoided because this would disrupt the system too much. For example, advocates of extra-sensory perception accuse the scientific community of unscientific practice with regard to the testing of this power. The possibility of extra-sensory perception is rejected because it does not cohere with the other propositions of the scientific community about recognized scientific practice.

Wittgenstein significantly remarked (*OC*, §§96–99):

> It might be imagined that some propositions, of the form of empirical propositions, were hardened and functioned as channels for such empirical propositions as were not hardened but fluid; and that this relation altered with time, in that fluid propositions hardened, and hardened ones became fluid.
>
> The mythology may change back into a state of flux, the river-bed of thoughts may shift. But I distinguish between the movement of the waters on the river-bed and the shift of the bed itself; though there is no sharp division of the one from the other.
>
> But if someone were to say 'So logic too is an empirical science' he would be wrong. Yet this is right: the same proposition may get treated at one time as something to test by experience, at another as a rule of testing.
>
> And the bank of that river consists partly of hard rock, subject to no alteration or only to an imperceptible one, partly of sand, which now in one place now in another gets washed away or deposited.

This analogy about the bed (world picture) and the waters (empirical propositions) of a river provided an illustration of the ideas that core propositions constitute our world picture, and that there is no sharp division between these propositions and the empirical ones (*OC*, §§95–99). What was part of the world picture against which we came to acquire other knowledge can shift and become part of the empirical propositions being tested. For example, in normal circumstances no sane person doubts how many hands they have (world picture) but I might wake up dazed after a terrible accident and wonder whether my hands which I cannot feel are still there or not (empirical proposition). A world picture proposition may take on the role of an empirical one and vice versa. It follows that some world picture propositions are only relatively certain. However, some others, such as 'that the earth exists', are absolutely certain. Wittgenstein's views about the status of world picture propositions differed from the positions of Descartes and Moore that all foundational propositions hold absolutely. Wittgenstein's stress on the relativistic character of foundationalism suggests the aptness of naming his position as relative foundationalism. However, the use of foundationalism might be questioned in so far as that term is frequently opposed to holism because there certainly are holistic tendencies in his remarks about a world picture being a system of propositions.

Stroll claims that as Wittgenstein's ideas progressed in *On Certainty* he gradually favoured absolute foundationalism over relative foundationalism. Wittgenstein abandoned the principles of relative foundationalism that world picture propositions form a system and that some of these propositions are only relatively certain. The absolute foundationalism is rather hinted at than explicitly stated. Absolute foundationalism held that some world picture propositions, such as 'that the earth exists', are absolutely certain (*OC*, §209). This position is that foundational propositions do not comprise a system and the foundations it describes are absolutist in character. Absolute foundationalism is developed by Wittgenstein in three directions. One is that certainty is something primitive, instinctual or animal (*OC*, §475). Another is that certainty is manifested in human action (*OC*, §§110, 196 and 204). The third is that certainty derives from training in communal practices (*OC*, §§170, 374 and 509).

It is worth observing that Wittgenstein also had a clear strategy against scepticism that goes right back to his early work in its essentials (*TLP*, §6.51). This was a Kantian anti-sceptical strategy as it dealt with scepticism by considering the bounds of sense.

RELIGION AND ETHICS

Wittgenstein once claimed that he saw every problem from a religious point of view and it is clear that he respected sincere religious conviction. His treatment of religion has been the subject of controversy both with regard to its nature and applications to questions in the philosophy of religion. There has been profound disagreement about how to handle Wittgenstein's writings in this area and they have been the topic of significant dispute. At present there is no consensus over the direction that should be taken. Some Wittgenstein scholars reject what appears to be the main philosophical message found in the remarks on magic and religious belief even whilst they accept his claims about language in other areas of discourse. Wittgenstein's remarks on religious belief have had an influence which is quite disproportionate to their number. He wrote very little on the topic, and much of it comes from brief collections of remarks, notes others made of his lectures and records of fragments of his thought. In his later period, there are primarily the 'Remarks on Frazer's *Golden Bough*', the 'Lectures on Religious Belief' and occasional remarks in *Culture and Value*. It has been suggested that Wittgenstein's remarks on religion can lead to radically different perspectives on religious belief and to novel ways of understanding specific topics such as creation and freedom of the will, and to a new focus for debating the question of faith and reason. A Wittgensteinian approach to religion (usually referred to as a form of fideism) has impacted upon the philosophy of religion, religious studies and theology.

Many philosophers and theologians regard Wittgensteinian fideism (which is very basically the view that religion is only intelligible to those who participate in it) as essentially defining what his view of religion is. Significant disputes about the reading of Wittgenstein's work on religious topics arise from examining fideism because it is not clear that his work should be interpreted in this way. The fideist view is that religious language is only intelligible to those who participate in the religious form of life. Fully understanding the language of a religious believer cannot be separated from comprehending a religious form of life. This kind of understanding is about making sense of human beings. Religious language constitutes a distinct linguistic practice which non-participants in the form of life could not grasp and show to be incoherent or mistaken. For example, an atheist could not find religious language intelligible and much less offer criticisms of it. This position is a kind of fideism (as understood in its general sense) because having religious faith is a precondition for taking place in rational discussions of that faith. Religious concepts are only accessible to those who partake in the form of life that they are used in. Cognisance of a religious form of life is necessary in order to see what it means to apply the ideas of truth and falsehood to religion. Religious beliefs are distinct language games because they are not linked to what lies outside religion as what is justified to its justification. The justification for religious beliefs stops, and the attempt to find justification for religious belief is a case of not being aware of where to stop. Neither does it make sense to request proof of the validity of religious beliefs. The desire for a foundation for religion is an instance of seeking justifications beyond the point where they should be. If there are distinct religious language games which are only understandable to those who share in the form of life, it follows that anyone who does not partake in the relevant form of life cannot criticize these distinct religious language games. The desirability of this position for the defence of religious beliefs against criticism is obvious. A major strand of critical thought about the fideistic handling of religious language games is concerned with the consequences of this for how the notion of the form of life is viewed. There have been objections to what has been regarded as the excessive compartmentalization of the forms of social life involved in maintaining that there are distinct religious language games. A ground for these objections is that this excessive compartmentalization leads to the undesirable consequence that the language of distinct religious groups, such as different kinds of Christians, is incommensurable. Instead it has been argued that the implications of distinct religious language games do extend across the boundaries of the language game into assertions concerning matters which lie beyond them. As such religious language is not something which is isolated and sufficient in itself and what comprises evidence for the truth or reliability of certain claims is not completely peculiar to the context or activity being investigated.

The fideistic interpretation of Wittgenstein's remarks on religion have been related and compared with other positions in the philosophy of religion. One of the most important views in recent philosophy of religion is the approach of what is called reformed epistemology. Both fideism and reformed epistemology share the views that belief in God's existence is not an isolated belief, that it has a contingent connection to other beliefs about him, and to the wider practice of religion itself. However, reformed epistemology represents a metaphysically realist stance towards the existence of God whilst in fideism questions about this are only possible within the religious language game. A major difference between reformed epistemology and fideism centres around the sort of questioning of religious belief that is legitimate. Reformed epistemology permits a considerable amount of reflection about religious belief and the epistemological foundations of it. By contrast in fideism the very thought of analysing the nature and epistemic grounds of religious belief indicates a lack of proper comprehension about the character of religion.

A view which has significant affinities and dissimilarities with the fideistic interpretation of Wittgenstein's remarks upon religion is that of treating theology as grammar. It is argued that he was concerned with grammatical status of theological statements. On this view, for example, apparent metaphysical assertions or denials about the existence of God are in effect grammatical propositions about the use of the term 'God'. For an atheist this term has no legitimate employment and as such is equivalent to a refusal to operate within the boundaries of religious language games. A postulation that religious discourse is some kind of nonsense does not provide any information about reality of a supernatural or any other kind. It follows from the familiar point that grammar is arbitrary that this is really a decision not to talk in a certain way and is not a refutation of the believer's use of language. The position of regarding theology as grammar argues that Wittgenstein wished neither to side with the believer or the atheist but rather wished to clarify that religious language was making grammatical or conceptual claims rather than factual ones. It should be observed a commitment to the view that theological statements are grammatical in character allows that they may guide religious actions and sentiments as well as contributing to the clarification of periodic descriptive assertions about certain individuals or events. It has been maintained that a properly developed conception of theology as grammatical would assist in defending Wittgenstein against charges that he has mischaracterized the nature of religious discourse and failed to protect religious belief from rational criticism. However, it remains to be demonstrated that this is the case.

An alternative to the fideist position has been to interpret the remarks on religious belief through the ideas of *On Certainty* and the aim of this kind of work has been to demonstrate how Wittgenstein's philosophy of religion is consistent with themes he developed there. According to this position both believers and non-believers have a world picture which is based upon their form of life and each world picture is as much or as little justified as any other. However, this leaves open the difficult question of whether Wittgenstein should be interpreted as a radical relativist. It is claimed that he agreed with the idea of the factuality of religious belief but thought that believers and non-believers hold contrary beliefs. Allied to this is the idea that religious belief is the consequence of a kind of life. For example, consider his discussion of the expression 'I believe that there will be a last judgement'. If such an expression is not being employed to make a prediction about what will happen in the future it raises the matter of how it is actually being used. Wittgenstein remarked that (*LC*, p. 56):

> Here believing obviously plays much more this role: suppose we said that a certain picture might play the role of constantly admonishing me, or I always think of it. Here there would be an enormous difference between those people for whom the picture is constantly in the foreground, and others who just didn't use it at all.

The attitude to the last judgement displayed here accords with the tone of a considerable number of his other remarks about religious belief. The implication of his comments seems to be that of equating religious beliefs with employing religious concepts, and possessing the associated attitudes and feelings which their use implies. Arguably this comes out most clearly in his well-known comment that 'It strikes me that a religious belief could only be something like a passionate commitment to a system of reference' (*CV*, p. 64). The point being expressed here is that religious belief is an alignment of an entire life which is not subject to changing scientific results and different philosophical doctrines. However, this idea of construing religious belief as being akin to a passionate system of reference has the consequence that unlike adherence to the truth of an empirically testable proposition religious beliefs cannot be true or false. Wittgenstein also held the view that religious beliefs could neither be reasonable or unreasonable if being reasonable meant that they could or could not be justified. He commented that (*LC*, p. 58):

I would say, they are certainly not reasonable, that's obvious. 'Unreasonable' implies, with everyone, rebuke. I want to say: they don't treat this as a matter of reasonability. Anyone who reads the Epistles will find it said: not only that it is not reasonable, but that it is folly. Not only is it not reasonable, but it doesn't pretend to be.

The implication here is that what is unreasonable is those who defend or criticize religion on the basis of the presupposition that religious beliefs can be corroborated or falsified by evidence. Both these kinds of proponents and opponents of religion have mistakenly applied scientific thinking to it. Religious beliefs are not analogous to scientific theories and should not be accepted or rejected using the same evidential standards. Wittgenstein maintained that attempts to demonstrate the existence of God or immortality of the soul or other similar propositions were absurd. Indeed they were indicative of a deep misunderstanding of the nature of religious belief and of the role of claims concerning God or the afterlife in the language of religious believers. Wittgenstein's clear rejection of the model of science as one which should be applicable to religion lies at the root of a major interpretation of his remarks on magic and religion, namely that of expressivism. The expressivist view is that Wittgenstein was fundamentally opposed to the anthropologist James Frazer's representation of magical and religious beliefs as mistaken hypotheses and rituals as primitive attempts to achieve what science does. He aimed to criticize Frazer's idea that magic and religion were primitive science by stressing how ritual and belief were essentially expressive in nature. That is to say, magic and religion should not be regarded as seeking to characterize and control supernatural powers but rather as the expressions of attitudes and emotions. Taken as expressions of these kinds magic and religion are not mistaken attempts at genuine science and are natural manifestations of what it is to be human. However, recently it has been claimed that Wittgenstein's comments about magic in 'Remarks on Frazer's *Golden Bough*' do not really lend to support to the expressivist interpretation. Such objections raise broader questions about whether a general interpretation of Wittgenstein's view of religious belief should be framed in expressivist terms.

Some commentators argue that Wittgenstein has mischaracterized the nature and meaning of religious discourse. That is to say, he has misrepresented the content of religious beliefs because he denied that religious believers have a belief in the existence of a causally efficacious divine being. It is claimed by contrast that most religious believers mean by their religious expressions exactly what Wittgenstein denies they mean and that religious faiths, such as Christianity, contain an essential commitment to this very belief. Wittgenstein was explicitly opposed to a cosmological conception of God as First Cause. However, it has been suggested that some of his ideas about causation and related themes enable the development of a new understanding of what religious believers mean when they speak of God as creator of the world. These are taken in conjunction with the idea that Wittgenstein was more open to the notion of an arranging and redeeming God. On this kind of account believing in God as the creator of the world does not have to be understood rationalistically.

Wittgenstein wrote almost nothing on ethics in his later work with the exception of the 'Lecture on Ethics' in 1929. In it ethics was regarded as covering everything that has value and concerning the meaning of life including aesthetics. However, the understanding and analysis of ethical problems was not discussed. Wittgenstein largely reiterated the view of the *Tractatus* that ethics is an attempt to say what cannot be said. He remarked that 'My whole tendency and I believe the tendency of all men who ever tried to write or talk on Ethics or Religion was to run against the boundaries of language' (*LE*, pp. 11f.). Wittgenstein tried to clarify the fact that his own attitude to ethics was different from a positivist attitude towards it. He commented ethics 'is a document of a tendency in the human mind which I personally cannot help respecting deeply and I would not for my life ridicule it' (*LE*, p. 12). Ethics is ineffable but the inclination to talk nonsense indicated something significant. Wittgenstein regarded ethics as of the utmost importance and as is evident from his diaries and the records of his conversations he thought a great deal about ethical problems. Some commentators have claimed that Wittgenstein believed that there is really nothing to say about ethics and therefore wrote increasingly little about it. This evidence of a clear interest in ethical problems suggests that this is an oversimplification.

In the 'Lecture on Ethics' Wittgenstein distinguished a relative from an ethical sense of terms of appreciation. A factual statement can never be or logically imply an ethical judgement of value, such as the obligation to keep promises. He invoked three experiences, including wondering at the existence of the world (*LE*, p. 11), to shed light on ethical value. Wittgenstein claimed that what tends to be said after such experiences misuses language but the experiences themselves 'seem to those who have had them, for instance to me, to have in some sense an intrinsic absolute value'. They cannot be expressed by factual statements since their value transcends the factual world (*LE*, pp. 7–9). However, later on Wittgenstein undertook some fragmentary investigations into the use of ethical terms (*AWL*, pp. 34–6 and *RPPI*, §160). He claimed that the meaning of the word 'good' is tied up with the act it qualifies (*AWL*, p. 35). Wittgenstein maintained that good is a family resemblance term. He remarked (*PG*, p. 77):

> Thus it could be said that the use of the word 'good' (in an ethical sense) is a combination of a very large number of inter-related games, each of them as it were a facet of the use. What makes a single concept here is precisely the relationship between these facets.

However, these investigations are too limited to allow significant conclusions about Wittgenstein's perspective on the grammatical rules governing ethical terms. There have been a number of applications of Wittgenstein's philosophical ideas to ethical problems. A classic example is von Wright's *The Varieties of Goodness* which exhibits and surveys the complex conceptual connections arising from the concept of good. This work illuminates the closely linked strands, such as those between the goodness of acts and intentions, of what he termed the 'the varieties of goodness'. More recently the employment of Wittgenstein's ideas to tackle ethical questions has become an identifiable kind of approach in moral philosophy. A representative example of this body of work is Paul Johnson's *Wittgenstein and Moral Philosophy*. However, for reasons considered in Chapter 5 there are grounds for thinking that the success of this approach is potentially limited.

AESTHETICS

Wittgenstein only discussed aesthetics in his 1938 'Lectures on Aesthetics'. The lectures have more similarities with his treatment of other philosophical questions, such as those about the mind, than one might think. Indeed these lectures are not so different because

Wittgenstein used ideas which are present in his other writings, such as the comparison of language to a tool chest (*LC*, p. 1) and many of the examples, like that of behaviourism (*LC*, p. 33), appear in other contexts in his work. Wittgenstein advocated the application of his philosophical methodology to aesthetic questions (*LC*, p. 28). He opposed the construction of philosophical theories about aesthetics, such as those about the nature of aesthetic judgement. Instead Wittgenstein sought to describe and clarify the character of aesthetic appreciation. For example, he claimed that he did not have a theory about the deterioration of taste and what he was doing was describing examples of this deterioration (*LC*, p. 10).

In the 'Lectures' Wittgenstein remarked that 'the subject (Aesthetics) is very big and entirely misunderstood' (*LC*, p. 1). The word 'beautiful' is frequently used adjectivally and the 'linguistic form of sentences' misleads one into thinking that beauty is an objective quality in objects (*LC*, p. 1). This point could be regarded as a criticism of the seventeenth-century conception of aesthetic appreciation which focused upon the beautiful qualities of an object (as from the eighteenth century onwards this conception became far less prevalent). Wittgenstein stressed that there was more to aesthetics than just appreciating the beauty of an object. A recurrent theme in the first lecture is the irrelevance of the use of aesthetic adjectives, such as 'lovely', 'marvellous' and 'fine'. Wittgenstein claimed that in real life aesthetic judgements hardly utilize aesthetic adjectives (*AWL*, p. 36 and *LC*, p. 3). He is surely mistaken about this as employing aesthetic adjectives is a familiar and natural way of expressing the impact of art. For example, a feeling of wonder at a work of art is often conveyed through aesthetic adjectives. Expressing such impact is part of genuinely appreciating art and a measure of the true importance of art. Indeed, Wittgenstein himself did use aesthetic adjectives to express his reactions to art so his own practice belied his professed position. For instance, this employment of aesthetic adjectives can be seen in his numerous remarks about art in *Culture and Value*. It is worth observing that had he construed the use of aesthetic adjectives as forms of aesthetic reaction, Wittgenstein would not have repeatedly minimized their role in aesthetics. He criticized a tendency to put too much emphasis upon aesthetic judgements about beauty to the detriment of other sorts of aesthetic judgements. Wittgenstein claimed that when a work of art is assessed it is more as either right or wrong than as beautiful or otherwise. Judgements of correctness employ words akin to 'right' and 'correct' (*AWL*, p. 36 and *LC*, p. 3). For example, he commented that 'in certain styles in Architecture a door is correct and the thing is you appreciate it' (*LC*, p. 8). Despite the sheer diversity of aesthetic appreciation what is primarily required for it is the learning of rules. This learning is a necessary but not sufficient condition for aesthetic appreciation for in its absence it would not be possible to articulate aesthetics responses (*LC*, p. 6). Wittgenstein considered the understanding derived from learning the rules more fundamental than any kind of spontaneous emotional response. Indeed in the 'Lectures' he regularly dismissed the idea that pure emotional response has a central role in aesthetic appreciation. Wittgenstein's concept of appreciation was more extensive than just that of judging correctness. He drew attention to the vast variety of cases that appreciation encompassed. These included ones in which an individual responded to a work of art because it 'makes a profound impression on him' (*LC*, p. 9). Another instance was that of the notion of the tremendous in art. Wittgenstein remarked (*LC*, pp. 7f.): 'When we talk of a Symphony of Beethoven we don't talk of correctness. Entirely different things enter. One wouldn't talk of appreciating the *tremendous* things in Art'. In passing, it is worth observing that the idea of the tremendous is significant for aesthetics and it is intriguing why Wittgenstein having raised the issue did not give it greater attention in the lectures.

Wittgenstein thought that it was an error to neglect the use of aesthetic expressions in favour of their linguistic form. Attention should not be focused on how aesthetic terms appear but upon the circumstances of their employment. Their usage is partly determined by the reasons which might be offered for their application. Aesthetic terms replace and extend natural reactions such as gestures of satisfaction or disapproval (*LC*, p. 2). Aesthetic appreciation takes a wide variety of forms including emotional affect and can be expressed as frequently by actions as by language. For example, running away from a house someone builds for us and refusing to live in it might be regarded as a criticism of the house (*LC*, p. 13). Wittgenstein claimed that the concept of aesthetic appreciation cannot be given a definition which provides the necessary and sufficient conditions for its employment. The different forms of aesthetic appreciation do not have any properties in common which ensure that the same concept is applied to all of them. He remarked

(*LC*, p. 7): 'It is not only difficult to describe what appreciation consists in, but impossible. To describe what it consists in we would have to describe the whole environment'. In the 'Lectures' Wittgenstein argued that aesthetic appreciation was essentially connected with forms of life. It is not possible to truly appreciate a work of art without assuming the form of life embodied in the culture of that work. In that sense, a particular instance of aesthetic judgement may not be entirely independent of moral or other kinds of values. Wittgenstein claimed that in 'order to get clear about aesthetic words you have to describe ways of living' (*LC*, p. 11). For instance, in the case of music appreciating it 'is a manifestation of human life' (*CV*, p. 80).

Wittgenstein argued that the tendency to separate aesthetic judgement from other cultural phenomena and practices was mistaken (*LC*, p. 2). He stressed that aesthetic appreciation is culturally determined and historically specific. Many examples of this view are found in the 'Lectures' and *Culture and Value*. Wittgenstein commented (*CV*, p. 96): 'I think that, in order to enjoy a poet, you have to *like* the culture to which he belongs as well. If you are indifferent to this or repelled by it, your admiration cools off'. He argued that a certain form of aesthetic appreciation is rendered possible and given meaning by the whole culture of a period. Wittgenstein illustrated this point with the case of Buffon who made very fine distinctions between words like 'grand', 'charming', 'nice'. He claimed that such distinctions can only be vaguely understood nowadays but Buffon meant them precisely. These nuances of meaning are possible and significant only within the culture in which Buffon lived (*LC*, p. 8). Another example is that the description of a 'cultured taste' required the description of a culture (*LC*, p. 8). Wittgenstein regarded contemporary forms of aesthetic appreciation as manifesting a deterioration in taste (*LC*, p. 7). His claims about the decline of taste introduce a potential tension into his remarks because judgements of this kind invoke the idea of aesthetic standards which are independent of particular cultural phenomena and practices. However, as has just been observed, Wittgenstein suggested that there could be no such standards.

Wittgenstein employed his distinction between philosophy and science when he claimed that scientific and especially psychological investigations were not relevant to aesthetics. However, he went further than this and criticized what he saw as the pernicious influence of that which he termed the idol worship of 'Science and the Scientist' on thinking about aesthetics (*LC*, p. 27). Wittgenstein claimed that it was mistaken to treat aesthetics as 'a kind of science' (*LC*, p. 11). He was referring to empirical science which uses experiments to determine causal relationships and frames explanations in causal terms. This objection to regarding aesthetics as a sort of science might appear to be a criticism of a position which has virtually never been advocated. However, what seems to motivate this mention of science was the more specific and major criticism that it was an error to treat aesthetics as 'a branch of psychology' (*LC*, p. 17). If aesthetics were regarded as part of psychology the study of it would concentrate upon the causal mechanisms which link mental phenomena to their behavioural manifestations with the aim of establishing generalizations about these connections. Wittgenstein conducted some psychological experiments on the role and importance of rhythm in music in 1912. It seems probable that these experiments were motivated by questions about aesthetics. It is possible that his remarks about aesthetics not being part of psychology were an oblique criticism of this earlier activity. However, it is evident that Wittgenstein's rejection of this approach to aesthetics had affinities with his criticism of the use of psychology in the philosophy of mind. Arguably, it is more plausible to think that his attitude to aesthetics was a special case of his more general one about the appropriate use and role of psychology.

For Wittgenstein, feelings are only relevant to aesthetic appreciation in so far as they constitute implicit aesthetic judgements. Different kinds of feelings are not specific to their objects and thus aesthetic feelings should not be seen as a special kind of feeling (*LC*, p. 12). Wittgenstein considered aesthetic reactions as perhaps 'the most important thing in connection with aesthetics' (*LC*, p. 13). He thought that difficulties arose from failing to grasp the implications of the intentional relationship between an aesthetic reaction and the object it is directed at (*LC*, pp. 11–18). Wittgenstein claimed that aesthetic feeling is the aesthetic reaction itself. He compared the feeling of discomfort as an aesthetic reaction to the drawing of one's hand away from a hot plate (*LC*, p. 14). The points of the comparison are to show that in reality the feeling and reaction are inseparable and that the feeling is directed at an object so the reaction constitutes a kind of criticism of that object. Wittgenstein held that an aesthetic reaction is a feeling which is directed towards an object in the form of a criticism (*LC*, p. 14). He criticised the view that aesthetic explanations are causal in nature (*LC*, p. 18) because this position claims that aesthetic reactions can be explained by discovering their mental causes. Wittgenstein illustrated his objection to the view that aesthetic reactions can be causally explained through consideration of some examples of psychoanalysis. He claimed that Freud's explanation of a dream in terms of certain elements does not demonstrate what the dream is actually about (*LC*, p. 23). The general point being made is that reductive explanations of this kind are not necessarily illuminating and may easily turn out to be misleading. Wittgenstein thought that aesthetic reactions had causes but that causes do not specify the reasons for these reactions. He held that consideration of causes is misguided and it is only pertinent to ask about reasons. This view is a specific case of Wittgenstein's general rejection of causal theories of intentionality. He referred to psychoanalysis more positively when he stated that, as with certain psychoanalytic explanations, characteristically an aesthetic explanation must command the assent of the individual who demands it (*LC*, p. 18). Aesthetic explanations account for reactions through enhancing understanding of the work of art itself and typically they have a descriptive form. Such explanations may involve straightforward reference to aesthetic standards but they can also succeed by indicating previously unseen connections. These connections indicate how and why particular artistic works have certain aesthetic qualities. For example, Wittgenstein remarked that he really appreciated Klopstock's poetry when he read it with an abnormally stressed metre (*LC*, p. 4). He applied the idea of family resemblance to aesthetics. Wittgenstein claimed that aesthetic terms cannot be given definitions which provide the necessary and sufficient conditions for their employment and that such terms are family resemblance ones (*LC*, p. 10). His position seems most convincing when applied to the terms 'art' and 'work of art'. There is no one condition by which objects qualify as art works. This application of family resemblance is Wittgenstein's most significant contribution to aesthetics and attempts to discover the essential nature of art have generally been relinquished.

Despite Wittgenstein's stress on misunderstandings in aesthetics he did offer a positive suggestion that art 'is based on the *concept* of the miracles of nature' (*CV*, p. 64). The connotations of this idea are that of having a sense of admiration and awe when appreciating a work of art. This experience of appreciation must somehow disclose the miraculous qualities of nature. Recognizing that Wittgenstein's aesthetic, religious and ethical thinking were connected in certain respects may help to elucidate the idea of the miracles of nature. For example, this notion of miraculous appears to be connected with his discussion of the experience of wondering at the existence of the world in the 'Lecture on Ethics' (p. 11). If so one possibility for understanding the conception of miraculous is that it is a way of seeing things and the adopting of a particular stance towards the world. Wittgenstein commented (*CV*, p. 64): '(The blossom, just opening out. What is *marvellous* about it?) We say: "Look, how it's opening out!" '. This remark seems to indicate that the distinction between saying and showing is relevant to the conception of miraculous because a miracle cannot really be expressed in language but can only be shown. Another aspect of this conception is that if one began to regard a miracle as a problem to be explained away then one would no longer be seeing the miraculous nature of the world. In such cases admiration for the miracles of nature 'will have suffered a rupture' (*CV*, p. 65). However, it remains unclear how art is grounded upon the idea of the miracles of nature.

NOTES

1 INTRODUCTION

1 Baker and Hacker (1992, pp. xxif.) supply a chronological ordering of this in so far as it is possible as some works cover many years.
2 The German title is *Logisch-Philosophische Abhandlung* and the English version was suggested by Moore in imitation of Spinoza's *Tractatus Theologico-Politicus*.
3 See von Wright (1979) for an illuminating discussion of this.
4 For details of editorial controversies about this work see Baker and Hacker (1976), Kenny (1984a) and Rhees (1996). The complete 'Big Typescript' was published in 2005.
5 For details see Hintikka (1991).
6 Ray Monk's *Ludwig Wittgenstein: The Duty of Genius* (1990) has been drawn upon for biographical details. Its bibliography has a good list of sources.
7 For details see Engelmann (1967).
8 For details see Fania Pascal's memoir (Luckhardt, 1979, pp. 28–30 and 40–42).
9 The discussion of language games in Chapter 4 and Wittgenstein's later philosophy of language in Chapter 6 should clarify why this is misuse.
10 The discussion of Wittgenstein's philosophical methodology (Chapter 5) and his later philosophy of language (Chapter 6) should provide insight into why it is a misrepresentation to read him in Derridean terms.

3 METAPHYSICS OF THE *TRACTATUS*

1 This remark introduces a term which is a potential source of confusion, namely *Sachverhalt*. Different translations give this as either a state of affairs (the literal one) or an atomic fact. For reasons of clarity the Ogden (1922) translation has been modified in places to incorporate the former rendering.

4 THE MIDDLE PERIOD

1 For further historical details on their evolving relationship see Baker (1979) and Waismann (2003).
2 Rhees made this claim on the title page of the *Blue and Brown Books*.
3 There is only one occurrence (§67) of the phrase 'family resemblance' in the *Investigations*.

5 AIMS AND METHODS OF PHILOSOPHICAL THERAPY

1 Waismann's and Wisdom's ideas in *Philosophy and Psycho-Analysis* have affinities. A detailed development of the claim that Waismann's conception of philosophical methodology should be attributed to Wittgenstein is given by Baker in *Neglected Aspects*.

6 PHILOSOPHY OF LANGUAGE AND MATHEMATICS

1 See Chapter 7 for a discussion of private language.
2 A less sophisticated analysis of this language game is found in the *Philosophical Grammar* (p. 57).
3 It is worth observing that his view could be objected to on the grounds that separate justification is required for the idea that the appropriate way to distinguish between syntax and semantics is to consider their relationship to arbitrary linguistic rules.
4 A well-known development of this strand is Winch's *The Idea of a Social Science* which characterizes the nature of social science.

7 PHILOSOPHY OF MIND

1 Only selected aspects of the private language argument will be covered. Given the vast secondary literature on this a comprehensive discussion is not possible here.
2 Some writings which espouse this view are Hacker (1986, Chapter IX) and Kenny (1983 Chapter 10, 1966, 1984b).
3 For the private language argument to be specifically directed against Cartesian dualism a focus on clear and distinct perception is required. However, the differentiation between sensation and perception was not stressed by Wittgenstein. (For an example of this see *PI*, §275.) This suggests that this interpretation is rather less plausible than the broader target of the Cartesian conception of the mind.
4 Presentation up to §258 is sufficient to indicate the viability of this handling of the argument since it can plausibly be thought that this section contains the core of the private language argument.
5 It is worth noting here that the concept of introspection should be clearly distinguished from other notions in the philosophy of mind.

Introspection is a vague notion and if the idea is used without elucidation or as a synonym for concepts, such as privileged access or immediate private experience, then this employment is insufficiently clear. The notion of introspection in itself is not necessarily problematic philosophically and what makes it so are the other view(s) which it is associated with. For example, the idea of introspection in conjunction with various epistemological postulates about how the mental can be known leads towards a privileged access perspective.

SELECT BIBLIOGRAPHY

SUGGESTIONS FOR FURTHER READING

The *Tractatus* should be read first followed by the *Investigations*. The *Blue and Brown Books* are usefully considered in conjunction with this latter work. After that *On Certainty* deserves attention. *Remarks on the Philosophy of Psychology*, *Remarks on the Foundations of Mathematics* and *Lectures and Conversations on Aesthetics, Psychology and Religious Beliefs* are well worth consulting.

The secondary literature on Wittgenstein is voluminous and it is very selectively covered here. The last major guide to the literature, *Wittgenstein: A Bibliographical Guide* (edited by Frongia and McGuinness), appeared in 1990. The best bibliographical source is the database *Philosopher's Index* which is available in major research and university libraries.

WITTGENSTEIN'S PUBLISHED WORKS

AWL *Wittgenstein's Lectures: Cambridge 1932–5* (1979). Ambrose, A. (ed.). Oxford: Basil Blackwell.

BB The *Blue and Brown Books* (1972). Oxford: Basil Blackwell.

CV *Culture and Value* (1977). von Wright, G.H. (ed.). Oxford: Basil Blackwell.

L *Wittgenstein's Lectures: Cambridge 1930–2* (1980). Lee, D. (ed.). Oxford: Basil Blackwell.

LC *Lectures and Conversations on Aesthetics, Psychology and Religious Beliefs* (1970). Barrett, C. (ed.). Oxford: Basil Blackwell.

LE 'A Lecture on Ethics' (1965). *Philosophical Review* 74, 3–12.

LFM *Wittgenstein's Lectures on the Foundations of Mathematics, Cambridge 1939* (1976). Diamond, C. (ed.). Sussex: Harvester Press.

LWCL *Ludwig Wittgenstein: Cambridge Letters* (1995). McGuinness, B.F. and von Wright, G.H. (eds.). Oxford: Basil Blackwell.

LWI *Last Writings on the Philosophy of Psychology vol. 1* (1982).

Nyman, H. and von Wright, G.H. (eds.). Aue, M.A.E. and Luckhardt, C.G. (trs.). Oxford: Basil Blackwell.

LWII *Last Writings on the Philosophy of Psychology vol. 2* (1993). Nyman, H. and von Wright, G.H. (eds.). Aue, M.A.E. and Luckhardt, C.G. (trs.). Oxford: Basil Blackwell.

NB *Notebooks 1914–1916* (1961). von Wright, G.H. and Anscombe, G.E.M. (eds.). Anscombe, G.E.M. (tr.). Oxford: Basil Blackwell.

OC *On Certainty* (1969). Anscombe, G.E.M. and von Wright, G.H. (eds.). Anscombe, G.E.M. and Paul, D. (trs.). Oxford: Basil Blackwell.

PG *Philosophical Grammar* (1974). Rhees, R. (ed.). Kenny, A.J.P. (tr.). Oxford: Basil Blackwell.

PI *Philosophical Investigations* (1984). Second edition. Anscombe, G.E.M. and Rhees, R. (eds.). Anscombe, G.E.M. (tr.). Oxford: Basil Blackwell.

PR *Philosophical Remarks* (1975). Rhees, R. (ed.). White, R. and Hargreaves, R. (trs.). Oxford: Basil Blackwell.

RFM *Remarks on the Foundations of Mathematics* (1967). von Wright, G.H., Rhees, R. and Anscombe, G.E.M. (eds.). Anscombe, G.E.M. (tr.). Oxford: Basil Blackwell.

RPPI *Remarks on the Philosophy of Psychology vol. 1* (1980). Anscombe, G.E.M. and von Wright, G.H. (eds.). Anscombe, G.E.M. (tr.). Oxford: Basil Blackwell.

RPPII *Remarks on the Philosophy of Psychology vol. 2* (1980). Nyman, H. and von Wright, G.H. (eds.). Aue, M.A.E. and Luckhardt, C.G. (trs.). Oxford: Basil Blackwell.

TLP *Tractatus Logico-Philosophicus* (1922). Ogden, C.K. (tr.). London: Routledge and Kegan Paul.

WWK *Ludwig Wittgenstein und der Wiener Kreis* (1967). Shorthand notes recorded by Waismann, F., McGuinness, B.F. (ed.). Oxford: Basil Blackwell.

Z *Zettel* (1967). Anscombe, G.E.M. and von Wright, G.H. (eds.). Anscombe, G.E.M. (tr.). Oxford: Basil Blackwell.

'Cause and Effect: Intuitive Awareness' (1993). In *Philosophical Occasions 1912–1951*, Klagge, J. and Norman, A. (eds.). Winch, P. (tr.). Indianapolis and Cambridge: Hackett Publishing, 370–405.

Eine Philosophische Betrachtung (1970). In Rhees, R. (ed.). *Ludwig Wittgenstein: Schriften 5*. Frankfurt: Suhrkamp, 117–237.

Philosophical Occasions 1912–1951 (1993). Klagge, J. and Norman, A. (eds.). Indianapolis and Cambridge: Hackett Publishing.

Prototractatus– An Early Version of Tractatus Logico– Philosophicus (1971). McGuinness, B.F., Nyberg, T. and von Wright, G.H. (eds.). Pears, D.F. and McGuinness, B.F. (trs.). London: Routledge and Kegan Paul.

Remarks on Colour (1977). Anscombe, G.E.M. (ed.). McAlister, L.L. and Schattle, M. (trs.). Oxford: Basil Blackwell.

'Remarks on Frazer's *Golden Bough*' (1979). In *Wittgenstein Sources and Perspectives*, Luckhardt, C.G. (ed.). Beversluis, J. (tr.). New York: Harvester Press, 61–81.

'Some Remarks on Logical Form' (1929). *Proceedings of the Aristotelian Society*, suppl. vol. 9, 162–171.

The Big Typescript: TS 213 (2005). Luckhardt, C.G. and Aue, M.A.E. (trs. and eds.). Oxford: Basil Blackwell.

'Wittgenstein's Lectures in 1930–33' (1959a). In Moore, G.E. *Philosophical Papers*. London: Allen and Unwin, 252–324.

Wittgenstein's Lectures on Philosophical Psychology 1946–47 (1988). Geach, P.T. (ed.). New York: Harvester Wheatsheaf.

'Wittgenstein's Notes for Lectures on "Private Experience" and "Sense Data"' (1993). In *Philosophical Occasions 1912–1951*, Klagge, J. and Norman, A. (eds.). Indianapolis and Cambridge: Hackett Publishing, 202–88.

Wittgenstein Gesamtbriefwechsel (2004). InteLex.

Wittgenstein's Nachlass: The Bergen Electronic Edition (2000). Oxford: Oxford University Press.

BACKGROUND AND BIOGRAPHY

Hacker, P.M.S. (1996b). *Wittgenstein's Place in Twentieth Century Analytic Philosophy*.

Kenny, A. (1995). *Frege*.

Malcolm, N. (1984). *Ludwig Wittgenstein: A Memoir*.

McGuinness, B. (1988). *Wittgenstein, a Life: Young Ludwig 1889–1921*.

Monk, R. (1990). *Ludwig Wittgenstein: The Duty of Genius*.

—— (1996). *Bertrand Russell: The Spirit of Solitude*.

INTRODUCTIONS

Fogelin, R. (1987). *Wittgenstein*.

Hacker, P.M.S. (1986). *Insight and Illusion: Themes in the Philosophy of Wittgenstein*.

Kenny, A. (1983). *Wittgenstein*.

Malcolm, N. (1986). *Nothing is Hidden: Wittgenstein's Criticism of his Early Thought*.

Schulte, J. (1992). *Wittgenstein: an Introduction*.

COLLECTIONS OF ARTICLES

Canfield, J. (ed.) (1986). *The Philosophy of Wittgenstein: A Fifteen Volume Collection*.

Griffiths, A. (ed.) (1991). *Wittgenstein: Centenary Essays*.

Shanker, S. (ed.) (1986). *Wittgenstein: Critical Assessments*.

EARLY WORK

Black, M. (1967). *A Companion to Wittgenstein's Tractatus*.

Griffin, J. (1964). *Wittgenstein's Logical Atomism*.

Mounce, H. (1981). *Wittgenstein's Tractatus: an Introduction.*
Pears, D.F. (1987). *The False Prison vol. 1.*

LATER WORK

Four-volume commentary on the *Philosophical Investigations*:
Baker, G.P. and Hacker, P.M.S. (1980). *Wittgenstein: Meaning and Understanding.*
Baker, G.P. and Hacker, P.M.S. (1992). *Rules, Grammar and Necessity.*
Hacker, P.M.S. (1990). *Wittgenstein: Meaning and Mind.*
Hacker, P.M.S. (1996a). *Wittgenstein: Mind and Will.*
Budd, M. (1989). *Wittgenstein's Philosophy of Psychology.*
Marion, M. (1998). *Wittgenstein and Finitism.*
Pears, D.F. (1988). *The False Prison vol. 2.*
Stroll, A. (1994). *Moore and Wittgenstein on Certainty.*

OTHER BOOKS AND ARTICLES RELEVANT TO WITTGENSTEIN

Addis, M. (1999). *Wittgenstein: Making Sense of Other Minds.* Aldershot: Ashgate.
Allen, R. and Turvey, M. (eds.) (2001). *Wittgenstein, Theory and the Arts.* London: Routledge.
Anscombe, G.E.M. (1959). *An Introduction to Wittgenstein's Tractatus.* London: Hutchison.
Arrington, R. and Addis, M. (eds.) (2001). *Wittgenstein and Philosophy of Religion.* London: Routledge.
——and Glock, H. (eds.) (1996). *Wittgenstein and Quine.* London: Routledge.
Baker, G.P. (1979). '*Verehrung und Verkehrung:* Waismann and Wittgenstein'. In Luckhardt, C.G. (ed.). *Wittgenstein: Sources and Perspectives.* Ithaca: Cornell University Press, 243–85.
—— (1999). 'Italics in Wittgenstein'. *Language and Communication* 19, 181–211.
—— (2002). 'Quotation-marks in *Philosophical Investigations* Part I'. *Language and Communication* 22, 37–68.
—— (2004). *Neglected Aspects.* Oxford: Basil Blackwell.
—— and Hacker, P.M.S. (1976). 'Critical notice: *Philosophical Grammar*, by Ludwig Wittgenstein'. *Mind* 85, 269–94.
—— and Hacker, P.M.S. (1980). *Wittgenstein: Meaning and Understanding.* Oxford: Basil Blackwell.
—— and Hacker, P.M.S. (1984). *Language, Sense and Nonsense.* Oxford: Basil Blackwell.
—— and Hacker, P.M.S. (1992). *Rules, Grammar and Necessity.* Oxford: Basil Blackwell.
Bennett, M.R. and Hacker, P.M.S. (2003). *Philosophical Foundations of Neuroscience.* Oxford: Basil Blackwell.
Black, M. (1967). *A Companion to Wittgenstein's Tractatus.* Ithaca: Cornell University Press.
Bloor, D. (2002). *Wittgenstein: Rules and Institutions.* London: Routledge.

Bouveresse, J. (1995). *Wittgenstein reads Freud*. Princeton: Princeton University Press.

Budd, M. (1989). *Wittgenstein's Philosophy of Psychology*. London: Routledge.

Canfield, J. (ed.) (1986). *The Philosophy of Wittgenstein: A Fifteen Volume Collection*. New York: Garland.

Copi, I. (1958). 'Objects, properties, and relations in the *Tractatus*'. *Mind* 67, 145–65.

Crary, A. and Read, R. (eds.) (2000). *The New Wittgenstein*. London: Routledge.

Engelmann, P. (1967). *Letters from Wittgenstein with a memoir*. Oxford: Basil Blackwell.

Fogelin, R. (1987). *Wittgenstein*. Second edition. London: Routledge.

Frege, G. (1962). *Grundgesetze der Arithmetic*. Hildesheim: Olms.

—— (1980). *Translations from the Philosophical Writings of Gottlob Frege*. Geach, P.T. and Black, M. (eds.). Black, M. *et al.* (trs.). Oxford: Basil Blackwell.

Frongia, G. and McGuinness, B.F. (eds.) (1990). *Wittgenstein: A Bibliographical Guide*. Oxford: Blackwell.

Gibson, J. and Huemer, W. (eds.) (2004). *The Literary Wittgenstein*. London: Routledge.

Griffin, J. (1964). *Wittgenstein's Logical Atomism*. Oxford: Oxford University Press.

Griffiths, A. (ed.) (1991). *Wittgenstein: Centenary Essays*. Cambridge: Cambridge University Press.

Hacker, P.M.S. (1986). *Insight and Illusion: Themes in the Philosophy of Wittgenstein*. Second edition. Oxford: Clarendon Press.

—— (1990). *Wittgenstein: Meaning and Mind*. Oxford: Basil Blackwell.

—— (1996a). *Wittgenstein: Mind and Will*. Oxford: Basil Blackwell.

—— (1996b). *Wittgenstein's Place in Twentieth Century Analytic Philosophy*. Oxford: Basil Blackwell.

Haller, R. (1988). *Questions on Wittgenstein*. London: Routledge.

Harre, R. and Tissaw, M. (2005). *Wittgenstein and Psychology: a Practical Guide*. Aldershot: Ashgate.

Hintikka, J. (1991). 'An impatient man and his papers'. *Synthese* 87, 183–201.

Johnson, P. (1989). *Wittgenstein and Moral Philosophy*. London: Routledge.

Kenny, A. (1966). 'Cartesian privacy'. In Pitcher, G. (ed.). *Wittgenstein: The Philosophical Investigations*. New York: Doubleday, 352–70.

—— (1983). *Wittgenstein*. Singapore: Penguin Books.

—— (1984a). 'From the *Big Typescript* to the *Philosophical Grammar*'. In *The Legacy of Wittgenstein*. Oxford: Basil Blackwell, 24–37.

—— (1984b). 'The first person'. In *The Legacy of Wittgenstein*. Oxford: Basil Blackwell, 77–87.

—— (1995). *Frege*. London: Penguin Books.

Kerr, F. (1997). *Theology after Wittgenstein*. London: SPCK.

Kripke, S. (1984). *Wittgenstein on Rules and Private Language*. Oxford: Basil Blackwell.

Lear, J. (1986). 'Transcendental anthropology'. In McDowell, J. and Pettit, P. (eds.). *Subject, Thought and Context*. Oxford: Clarendon Press, 267–98.

Luckhardt, C.G. (ed.) (1979). *Wittgenstein: Sources and Perspectives*. Ithaca: Cornell University Press.

Lyotard, J. (1984). *The Postmodern Condition: A Report on Knowledge*. Bennington, G. and Massumi, B. (trs.). Manchester: Manchester University Press.

Malcolm, N. (1984). *Ludwig Wittgenstein: A Memoir*. Oxford: Oxford University Press.

—— (1986). *Nothing is Hidden: Wittgenstein's Criticism of his Early Thought*. Oxford: Basil Blackwell.

—— (1994). *Wittgenstein: A Religious Point of View?* Winch P. (ed.). Ithaca: Cornell University Press.

Marion, M. (1998). *Wittgenstein and Finitism*. Oxford: Clarendon Press.

McDowell, J. (1981). 'Non-cognitivism and rule following'. In Holtzman, S. and Leich, C. (eds.). *Wittgenstein: to Follow a Rule*. London: Routledge and Kegan Paul, 141–62.

McGinn, M. (1989). *Sense and Certainty*. Oxford: Basil Blackwell.

McGuinness, B. (1988). *Wittgenstein, a Life: Young Ludwig 1889–1921*. London: Duckworth.

Monk, R. (1990). *Ludwig Wittgenstein: The Duty of Genius*. London: Jonathan Cape.

—— (1996). *Bertrand Russell: The Spirit of Solitude*. London: Jonathan Cape.

—— (2000). *Bertrand Russell: The Ghost of Madness*. London: Jonathan Cape.

Moore, G.E. (1959b). 'A defence of common sense'. In *Philosophical Papers*. London: Allen and Unwin, 32–59.

—— (1959c). 'Proof of the external world'. In *Philosophical Papers*. London: Allen and Unwin, 127–50.

—— (1959d). 'Certainty'. In *Philosophical Papers*. London: Allen and Unwin, 223–46.

Mounce, H. (1981). *Wittgenstein's Tractatus: an Introduction*. Oxford: Basil Blackwell.

Noe, A. (1994). 'Wittgenstein, phenomenology and what it makes sense to say'. *Philosophy and Phenomenological Research* 54, 1–42.

Pears, D.F. (1987). *The False Prison vol. 1*. Oxford: Oxford University Press.

—— (1988). *The False Prison vol. 2*. Oxford: Oxford University Press.

Rhees, R. (1996). 'On editing Wittgenstein'. *Philosophical Investigations* 19, 55–61.

Russell, B. (1903). *The Principles of Mathematics*. London: Allen and Unwin.

—— (1956a). 'Mathematical logic as based on the theory of types'. In Marsh, R.C. (ed.). *Logic and Knowledge, Essays 1901–1950*. London: Allen and Unwin, 59–102.

—— (1956b). 'On denoting'. In Marsh, R.C. (ed.). *Logic and Knowledge, Essays 1901–1950*. London: Allen and Unwin, 479–93.

—— (1956c). 'The philosophy of logical atomism'. In Marsh, R.C. (ed.).

Logic and Knowledge, Essays 1901–1950. London: Allen and Unwin, 175–281.

—— (1959). *My Philosophical Development.* London: Allen and Unwin.

—— (1967). *The Problems of Philosophy.* London: Oxford University Press.

—— and Whitehead, A.N. (1910–13). *Principia Mathematica.* Cambridge: Cambridge University Press.

Schopenhauer, A. (1966). *The World as Will and Representation.* Payne, E. (tr.). New York: Dover.

Schulte, J. (1992). *Wittgenstein: an Introduction.* New York: SUNY Press.

Shanker, S. (ed.) (1986). *Wittgenstein: Critical Assessments.* London: Croom Helm.

Staten, H. (1986). *Wittgenstein and Derrida.* Lincoln and London: University of Nebraska Press.

Stenius, E. (1960). *Wittgenstein's Tractatus: A Critical Exposition of its Main Lines of Thought.* Oxford: Blackwell.

Stroll, A. (1994). *Moore and Wittgenstein on Certainty.* Oxford: Oxford University Press.

von Wright, G.H. (1963). *The Varieties of Goodness.* London: Routledge and Kegan Paul.

—— (1979). 'The origin of Wittgenstein's *Tractatus*'. In Luckhardt, C.G. (ed.). *Wittgenstein: Sources and Perspectives.* Ithaca: Cornell University Press, 138–60.

Waismann, F. (1968). 'How I see philosophy'. In Harre, R. (ed.). *How I See Philosophy.* London: Macmillan, 1–38.

—— (1976). *Logik, Sprache, Philosophie.* Baker, G.P. and McGuinness, B. (eds.). Stuttgart: Reclam.

—— (1997). *The Principles of Linguistic Philosophy.* Second edition. Harre, R. (ed.). Basingstoke: Macmillan.

—— (2003). *The Voices of Wittgenstein.* Baker, G.P. (ed.). Baker, G.P. *et al.* (trs.). London: Routledge.

Winch, P. (1988). *The Idea of a Social Science and its Relation to Philosophy.* London: Routledge and Kegan Paul.

Wisdom, J. (1969). *Philosophy and Psycho-Analysis.* Berkeley and Los Angeles: University of California Press.

INDEX